Accounting: An Introduction for Professio

Accounting: An Introduction for Professional Students

JOHN DUNN

Pitman Publishing
128 Long Acre, London WC2E 9AN

A Division of Longman Group UK Limited

First published in 1992

© Longman Group UK Ltd 1992

A CIP record for this book is available from the British Library.

ISBN 0 273 03731 5

Printed in Great Britain by The Bath Press, Avon

For Richard, Iain, Andrew and Jonathan

Contents

Preface   ix

1   Double entry bookkeeping   **1**

The balance sheet equation   1
The dual aspect concept   5
'T' accounts   6
Making use of 'T' accounts   10

2   The profit and loss account and balance sheet   **16**

The trial balance   16
The profit and loss account   18
The balance sheet   21
Accounting for fixed assets   28
Other adjustments   38
Avoiding omissions   40

3   Published accounts   **47**

Regulations affecting the preparation of published accounts   48
Statutory formats   50
Notes to the accounts   60
Disclosure of accounting policies   76

4   Taxation in company accounts   **78**

The calculation of corporation tax   78
The payment of taxation   81
Dividends and advance corporation tax   87
Irrecoverable ACT   97
Deferred tax   104
Corporation tax in the financial statements   107

5   Consolidated financial statements   **115**

Basic concepts   116
The consolidated balance sheet   117
Pre-acquisition profits   118
Goodwill and capital reserves   123
Minority interests   128
Inter-company balances   133
Revaluation of assets on consolidation   139
Consolidated profit statement   145

6   Practical bookkeeping   **154**

Initial recording of transactions   154
Computerised systems   168

7   Interpretation of financial statements   **171**

Why calculate ratios?   171
The main accounting ratios   174
Some limitations of ratio analysis   190
Ratio analysis and the auditor   191

8   The cash flow statement   **194**

Financial Reporting Standard 1   194
The purpose of the statement   195
The form and content of the statement   195
Interpreting the statement   207
A variation on the basic question   213

Index   221

Preface

Introduction

Over 10% of the UK's graduates enter the accountancy profession. Becoming an accountant involves a further period of study and requires that yet another set of examinations be passed. Preparing for these exams can induce a sense of 'culture shock'.

Graduates from non-accounting backgrounds are suddenly confronted with unfamiliar jargon and a whole series of rules about the manner in which apparently unintelligible figures ought to be laid out.

Accounting graduates are not necessarily much better off. Professional accounting exams are not necessarily more difficult than those encountered at degree or diploma level, but they are designed to test different types of skill and knowledge. Most undergraduate courses cover the basics of accounting during the beginning of their first year and, quite properly, quickly move on to consider the conceptual aspects of accountancy. Qualified accountants do, of course, have to know about these. The professional bodies tend, however, to test the candidate's understanding of them by setting numerical questions which involve the application of these principles. The problem faced by the accounting graduate or diploma holder is that he or she may have the necessary theoretical knowledge but have forgotten a great deal of the simpler material which provides the context for these questions.

This book is intended to help students embarking on their professional courses by going over those aspects of basic accounting which tend to create difficulties, either because the material has been forgotten or because it has not been covered in the necessary depth at undergraduate level. It does so in as concise a manner as possible and places a great deal of emphasis on the development of a methodology for approaching each type of question covered. It is intended to supplement the traditional core reading or study manuals rather than replace them.

Coverage

The level of detail in each chapter has been pitched according to the likely needs of most readers. Chapter 1 looks at double entry bookkeeping, concentrating on its use as a means of simplifying various types of calculation. This is a fairly detailed chapter because many students complain that they remember little about the subject, or even that they have never properly understood it!

Chapters 2 and 3 cover the profit and loss account and balance sheet. Chapter 2 looks at the preparation of the basic statements and Chapter 3 provides an overview of the publication requirements with which companies must comply. These chapters concentrate quite heavily on the general approach which should be taken to questions involving the preparation of these statements. Chapter 3 is not intended to be exhaustive; it is intended to provide an introduction to a complicated area which will be developed by further reading.

Chapter 4 considers the problem of accounting for taxation. Those students who have been given exemptions from all but the final stage of their professional studies will, hopefully, benefit from the detailed description of the tax system and the manner in which the tax charge and liabilities are accounted for. Students who have taken the intermediate examinations may already be familiar with this topic. Some courses may take a fairly detailed knowledge of it for granted.

Chapter 5 introduces the topic of consolidations with a fairly detailed description of the acquisition method of accounting for groups. The approach which is suggested can be easily adapted to the other methods that are sometimes used.

Chapter 6 is of more direct interest to auditing students. It introduces the factors which must be taken into account when designing accounting systems. This material is largely ignored on accounting courses, but is almost taken for granted in auditing syllabuses.

Chapter 7 introduces the interpretation of accounting statements. It looks at the ratios which accountants often use to help them understand the material contained in a profit and loss account or balance sheet.

Chapter 8 deals with the cash flow statement. This is a relatively new statement which replaces the old statement of source and application of funds. This topic could be a fruitful source of examination questions.

How to use the book

Learning to prepare a set of accounting statements is rather like learning to drive: it is necessary to practise. Each chapter contains a number of 'illustrations'. These are intended to show how the material which has been described can be applied. It is important that they are worked through, almost literally line by line, to see where the figures have come from. They are supported by 'progress tests', which are designed to reinforce the learning process by giving the readers an opportunity to practise the techniques which they have read about. They are supposed to be attempted as they are reached within the chapter. Full solutions are provided. Readers should compare their answers with those in the book and consider whether any differences are due to error or simply a difference of opinion. The illustrations and progress tests should be supplemented by attempting similar questions from past examination questions and from any other books or manuals which are being used. A great deal of material has to be remembered and it is easier to learn it by practising than trying to memorise it during final revision.

It is important to develop good habits. Accountants are expected to be good communicators and marks may be deducted in the examination if an answer is badly laid out. More marks may be lost because the candidate's understanding of the material has been obscured. Methods of presenting answers clearly will be suggested throughout the book. It is unwise to adopt an untidy approach to answering practice questions and expect to produce a readable script in the examination itself.

1 Double entry bookkeeping

It is difficult to imagine a process which is simpler or more mechanical than double entry bookkeeping. It is, however, unfortunate that many students do not grasp its simple rules. The very simplicity of double entry makes it an ideal method for laying out complicated workings in an examination. Some of the complicated adjustments which feature in some questions can be simplified to such an extent that they require very little thought. It will be used for this purpose throughout this book and it is recommended that readers do not proceed from this chapter until they have become thoroughly acquainted with its contents.

Objectives

This chapter covers the following key topics:

- The balance sheet equation (see progress test 1)
- The dual aspect concept (see progress test 2)
- The updating of T accounts (see progress test 3)
- The uses of T accounts (see progress test 4)

The balance sheet equation

One of the accountant's duties is to summarise the financial position of the organisation for which he works. The organisation can be portrayed in terms of either the things which it owns or its financial commitments.

Everything which has value and is owned by a business is called an 'asset'.

A business has two different types of financial obligation. Any amount which has been invested by the owners, for example money paid for shares, is called 'capital'. Any amount which the business owes to someone other than its owners is called a 'liability'.

Taking these simple definitions at face value, there is an obvious relationship between them. The assets of the business must have been paid for somehow. The cost would either have been met from funds invested by the shareholders or by taking out a loan from a third party. This means that a summary of the business's financial position would reveal that:

Assets = Capital + Liabilities

This is known as 'the balance sheet equation'. Its truth may not be immediately apparent. A company could, for example, borrow money in order to mount an advertising campaign. If this money was spent but the campaign was unsuccessful then there would still be a liability in respect of the loan, but no corresponding asset. This would not, however, invalidate the balance sheet equation. This is because of the nature of the owners' capital.

In most companies, the owners' capital will be constantly changing. This is not just because the shareholders may make the occasional purchase of new shares or receive a payment of dividend from time to time. The owners of the company are entitled to all of the profits earned by the company and must also bear all of the associated risks. This means that their capital will be increased if the company makes a profit and reduced if it incurs a loss. In simplistic terms, profit is simply income less expenses. Thus, the owners' capital is increased by every transaction involving income and decreased by every expense. The balance sheet equation could be restated as follows:

Assets = Capital + Income − Expenses + Liabilities

or, adding expenses to both sides:

Assets + Expenses = Capital + Income + Liabilities

Progress Test 1

List the assets, liabilities and capital items for each of the following companies and prove the balance sheet equation.

(a) PQR Ltd

	£
Buildings	20,000
Machinery	11,000
Vehicles	14,000
Debtors	3,000
Cash at Bank	1,000
Creditors	2,000
Bank Loan	4,000
Shareholders' Investment	43,000

(b)   STU Ltd

	£
Long Term Loan	25,000
Land and Buildings	30,000
Balance at Bank (Overdraft)	11,000
Creditors	7,000
Debtors	9,000
Delivery Van	5,000
Shareholders' Investment	7,000
Stock	6,000

(c)   VWX Ltd

	£
Income from Sales	20,000
Creditors	8,000
Cash at Bank	9,000
Cost of Goods Purchased	12,000
Bank Interest Received	1,000
Loan	15,000
Interest Paid on Loan	2,000
Wages	10,000
Shareholders' Investment	11,000
Premises	22,000

Solution to Progress Test 1

(a)   Assets

	£
Buildings	20,000
Machinery	11,000
Vehicles	14,000
Debtors	3,000
Cash at Bank	1,000
	49,000

   Liabilities

	£
Creditors	2,000
Bank Loan	4,000
	6,000

	£
Shareholders' Investment	43,000

Assets = £49,000

Capital + Liabilities = £6,000 + 43,000 = £49,000

(b)   Assets

	£
Land and Buildings	30,000
Debtors	9,000
Delivery Van	5,000
Stock	6,000
	50,000

Liabilities

	£
Long Term Loan	25,000
Balance at Bank (Overdraft)	11,000
Creditors	7,000
	43,000

	£
Shareholders' Investment	7,000

Assets = £50,000

Capital + Liabilities = £7,000 + 43,000 = £50,000

(c)   Assets

	£
Cash at Bank	9,000
Premises	22,000
	31,000

Expenses

	£
Cost of Goods Purchased	12,000
Interest Paid on Loan	2,000
Wages	10,000
	24,000

Liabilities

	£
Creditors	8,000
Loan	15,000
	23,000

Income

	£
Income from Sales	20,000
Bank Interest Received	1,000
	21,000

	£
Shareholders' Investment	11,000

Assets + Expenses = £31,000 + 24,000 = £55,000

Capital + Income + Liabilities = £11,000 + 21,000 + 23,000 = £55,000

The dual aspect concept

Every transaction affects two balances in a company's records. This follows from the balance sheet equation. A new asset, for example, cannot appear from nowhere. Its acquisition must be paid for either from another investment or loan or by a payment made using another asset. Thus, if a company wished to purchase stock it could either buy it on credit, thereby increasing an asset and a liability by the same amount, or it could pay cash, thereby increasing one asset and reducing another.

Double entry bookkeeping derives its name from the fact that each of the two aspects of the transaction must be recorded, thus resulting in a 'double entry'.

Progress Test 2

Identify the changes which will have to be recorded in order to account for the following transactions:

1.   A vehicle was purchased, the company paid by cheque.
2.   Office furniture was purchased on credit.

3. Wages were paid in cash.
4. The company received interest on its bank deposit account.
5. A debtor paid for the goods which he had received during the preceding month.

Solution to Progress Test 2

1. Increase the asset of vehicles.
   Decrease the asset of bank.
2. Increase the asset of office furniture.
   Increase the liability of sundry creditors.
3. Increase the expense of wages.
   Decrease the asset of cash (or bank).
4. Increase the asset of bank.
   Increase the income of interest received.
5. Increase the asset of bank (or cash).
   Decrease the asset of debtors.

'T' Accounts

One of the reasons why double entry is misunderstood is the way in which simple concepts are described in terms of accounting terminology. This jargon is a useful means of describing certain actions and procedures succinctly. Its meaning must, however, be understood.

An 'account' is simply a record of the transactions relating to a particular balance. It is best to think of an account as a page in a book. There are only two possible types of change which can be made to a balance: it can either be increased or decreased. It helps, therefore, to rule each page down the middle and to show increases on one side and decreases on the other. In examinations, this can be laid out as follows:

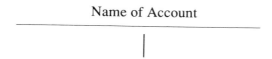

Name of Account

This is called a 'T' account because of the shape created by the lines when they intersect.

In practice, most accounting systems are computerised and accounts tend to be laid out differently on computer printouts. This does not mean that T accounts are old fashioned, it simply reflects the problems of programming a computer to print out data in the traditional format.

It has already been suggested that there are five different types of balance. These can be summarised as follows:

A   B
Assets   Capital
Expenses   Income
             Liabilities

The balances have been classified into two groups. Each group is the opposite of the other in bookkeeping terms. This is because an increase in an account in group A must be matched by either a decrease in another group A account or an increase in a group B account (and vice versa). Take a few minutes to think about this. Apply it to the transactions listed in progress test 2 and to any other simple transactions which come to mind. For example, the purchase of stock on credit increases the asset of stock (group A) and also the liability of creditors (group B).

The fact that the two groups of accounts are opposites means that their T accounts must be mirror-images of one another. This can be seen by looking at the way in which increases and decreases are recorded. By convention, an increase in an asset is recorded by writing the amount of the increase on the left hand side of its account. It follows that a decrease in an asset would be recorded on the right hand side. The opposite is true of liabilities: an increase is shown on the right hand side of the page and a decrease is shown on the left. Thus, the purchase of £100 of stock on credit would be shown as follows:

Stock (purchases)	Creditors
Creditors 100		Stock 100

Notice that each entry states the name of the account to which the corresponding entry has been posted. In practice, the date of the entry would be stated, along with further details to cross-reference the transaction to any related documents such as invoices or purchase orders. (In Chapter 2 we will see that there are usually two accounts for stock because sales and purchases have to be accounted for separately.)

It is cumbersome to write or speak about the left and right hand sides of the page and so the word 'debit' is used to describe the act of putting an entry on the left hand side of the page and 'credit' is used to refer to the process of making entries on the right. In the example outlined above, we have debited the Stock account with £100 and credited the Creditors account with the same amount.

This means that the whole of double entry can be summed up in the following table:

	Asset Expense	Capital Income Liability
Increases	Debit	Credit
Decreases	Credit	Debit

This can be simplified further by remembering that an increase in an asset or expense is recorded by a debit. Everything else can then be deduced from this. A decrease in one of these items must be recorded by a credit. An increase in capital, income or a liability must be recorded by a credit.

Progress Test 3

Identify the accounts which will have to be debited and credited in order to record each of the following transactions:

1. Bought a new machine for £5,000, paying by cheque.
2. Bought stock for £3,000 on credit.
3. Paid supplier £3,000 to settle balance.
4. Sold stock for £4,000 on credit terms.
5. Received £4,000 from debtors.
6. Paid rent of £2,000.
7. Received a royalty payment of £1,000.

Solution to Progress Test 3

1. Increase asset of machinery
   – Debit Machinery   £5,000
   Decrease asset of bank
   – Credit Bank   5,000
2. Increase asset of stock
   – Debit Purchases   £3,000
   Increase liability of creditors
   – Credit Creditors   3,000
3. Decrease liability of creditors
   – Debit Creditors   £3,000

	Decrease asset of bank		
	– Credit Bank		3,000
4.	Increase asset of debtors		
	– Debit Debtors	£4,000	
	Decrease asset of stock		
	– Credit Sales		4,000
5.	Increase asset of bank		
	– Debit Bank	£4,000	
	Decrease asset of debtors		
	– Credit Debtors		4,000
6.	Increase expense of rent		
	– Debit Rent	£2,000	
	Decrease asset of bank		
	– Credit Bank		2,000
7.	Increase asset of bank		
	– Debit Bank	£1,000	
	Increase income of royalties		
	– Credit Royalties		1,000

It is important to remember that each transaction has both a debit and a credit component. It is common to see the debit entry listed before the credit, although there may be times when it would be easier to think about the credit side first. If, for example, a transaction led to a decrease in the asset of bank then the bank account would have to be credited and it can be deduced from this that the other part of the entry would have to be a debit.

Journal Entries

It is normal practice to make a record of the details of any unusual or non-recurring entries to the accounts. This enables the accountant or an auditor to check the logic underlying the adjustment more easily. These notes are usually kept together in a diary or 'journal' and are referred to as 'journal entries'. It may be helpful to lay some workings out in the form of journal entries in examinations. These are easy for the examiner to follow and encourage a methodical approach to the solution of any complex adjustments in a question.

By convention, the debit entry relating to the transaction is stated first. This is followed by the credit entry and then a brief explanation of the journal. For example, the first transaction in Progress Test 3 would appear as follows:

Debit Machinery   £5,000
    Credit Bank   £5,000

Being the purchase of a new machine.

The Nominal Ledger and Trial Balance

The accounts will normally be kept together in a book (or a computer file) called a 'nominal' or 'general' ledger. This is best thought of as a loose-leaf binder containing a T account for every balance.

The balances on all of the accounts in the nominal ledger will be calculated at regular intervals and these will be listed in columnar form with separate columns for the debit and credit balances. This listing is called a 'trial balance'. The trial balance provides an arithmetical check on the application of double entry because the totals of the two columns of figures will only be equal if the debits and credits entered into the accounts agree. The trial balance does not, however, prove that the figures are correct. It would still square if, for example, both parts of an entry had been omitted from the ledger or if the wrong amount had been entered in both accounts.

The trial balance is a convenient summary of the balances on the ledger accounts for use in the preparation of the financial statements.

Examples of the trial balance will be introduced in Chapter 2.

Making use of 'T' accounts

It is, of course, extremely unlikely that any of the questions in an examination will be as basic as those which have been encountered so far. There are, however, two extremely important ways in which these accounts can be used to assist in workings.

Marshalling Information

It may be that several detailed figures have to be brought together in order to arrive at a figure which is to appear in a financial statement. While it will often be possible to calculate these figures using common sense, there will often be occasions where the sheer volume of data which are to be dealt with requires the methodical approach which double entry requires. This will be shown to best effect in Chapter 5 on consolidations.

Illustration 1

XYZ Ltd owed its creditors £10,000 at the beginning of the year. During the year, it purchased £140,000 of goods on credit and made payments of £125,000. How much was owed to creditors at the end of the year?

The T account for creditors would appear as follows:

Creditors

Bank	125,000	Balance brought down	10,000
Balance carried down	25,000	Purchases	140,000
	150,000		150,000
		Balance brought down	25,000

The opening balance was a liability and was shown as a credit. This liability was then increased by the purchases on credit and reduced by the payments made during the year. These transactions were, therefore, shown as a credit and a debit respectively.

Once the opening balance and the transactions were entered, the account had a total of £150,000 on the credit side (£10,000 + 140,000) and only £125,000 on the debit side. This meant that there was a balance of £25,000 (£150,000 – 125,000) on the credit side of the account. This credit balance represents the amount owed to creditors at the year end.

Notice that the opening balance is referred to as the 'Balance brought down' (usually abbreviated to Bal b/d) and the closing balance is the 'Balance carried down' (Bal c/d). Once the closing balance has been calculated and entered, the two columns are totalled as an arithmetical check to prove that both sides now agree. The closing balance is written below the totals to signify the fact that this balance will remain in the records until it is altered by further transactions.

The problem of prepaid and accrued expenses can also be dealt with using a T account. Prepayments occur whenever a company has to pay for an expense in advance. Any amount of the payment which relates to the following accounting period should be identified at the year end and carried forward as an asset. The expense incurred during the year is the amount of the asset or service which has actually been consumed during the year. The same applies to accruals. If an expense is paid in arrears, any amount which has been consumed but not yet recorded should be estimated and recorded as a liability at the year end.

Illustration 2

JKL Ltd had prepaid £200 of its insurance premium at 31 December 19X5. £3,000 was paid to the insurance company during the year ended 31 December 19X6. £300 of the payments made during the year were in respect of the year ended 31 December 19X7. What was the cost of insurance for the year ended 31 December 19X6 ?

Insurance

Bal b/d	200	Profit and Loss	?
Bank	3,000	Bal c/d	300
	3,200		3,200
Bal b/d	300		

The insurance account can be made to balance by inserting the figure of £2,900. This is the cost of insurance incurred during the year.

Incomplete Records

It is quite common for examiners to give information in a disguised form. This is a test of understanding. The missing figure can often be inferred by inserting the details given in the question into an account and calculating the balancing figure.

Illustration 3

The debtors of ABC Ltd owed £50,000 at the beginning of the year. During the year, the debtors paid a total of £450,000. At the end of the year, balances totalling £60,000 were outstanding. What was the value of sales on credit for the year?

While it would not be difficult to calculate this figure with the aid of some simple algebra, the figure could be derived more easily and with less risk of error by means of a T account for debtors.

Debtors

Bal b/d	50,000	Bank	450,000
Sales	?	Bal c/d	60,000
	510,000		510,000
Bal b/d	60,000		

This account does not balance because the figure for sales is missing. Both sides should total to £510,000, while the debit side amounts to only £50,000. This could be remedied by assuming that credit sales for the year amounted to £460,000 (i.e. £510,000 – 50,000).

Progress Test 4

1. The repairs account had a credit balance of £500 brought forward at 1 January 19X4 in respect of repairs made to plant during the year ended 31 December 19X3.

    The bank records reveal that a total of £18,000 was paid to contractors for repairs during the year ended 31 December 19X4.

    It was discovered that £2,000 of the amount recorded in respect of repairs had been allocated to the wrong heading. The payment should have gone to purchases.

    A further sum of £1,500 was owed to contractors at 31 December 19X4.

    Prepare a T account which shows the cost of repairs for the year ended 31 December 19X4.

2. The rental agreement on the office photocopier requires that the company pay in advance for the rental of the machine on a quarterly basis. In addition, the company is required to pay a small fee which is based on the number of copies made – as measured by a meter on the machine.

    At the beginning of the year, the company had paid £50 in advance rentals and owed £80 in respect of copies which had been taken but not yet paid for.

    The bank records show that the company paid £3,000 to the owner of the copier during the year.

    At the end of the year, £60 had been paid in advance for rentals and £100 is owed in respect of copies.

    Prepare a T account which shows the total cost of photocopying for the year.

3. At the beginning of the year, DEF Ltd's debtors owed £6,000. During the year, the customers made total payments of £80,000. Discounts of £3,000 were given and a debt worth £1,000 was written off as being uncollectable. Balances worth £7,000 were outstanding at the end of the year.

    The company owed its creditors £4,000 at the beginning of the year. During the year, it made payments of £50,000 to its suppliers. At the end of the year, it still owed £5,000.

Prepare T accounts for debtors and creditors and use these to derive figures for credit sales and purchases.

Solution to Progress Test 4

1.

Repairs			
Bank	18,000	Bal b/d	500
		Purchases	2,000
Bal c/d	1,500	Profit and Loss	?
	19,500		19,500
		Bal b/d	1,500

A balancing figure of £17,000 must be entered, this being the cost of repairs.

2.

Photocopier			
Bal b/d	50	Bal b/d	80
Bank	3,000	Profit and Loss	?
Bal c/d	100	Bal c/d	60
	3,150		3,150
Bal b/d	60	Bal b/d	100

The balancing figure is £3,010, which is the cost of photocopying for the year.

3.

Debtors			
Bal b/d	6,000	Bank	80,000
Bank	3,000	Discounts	3,000
Sales	?	Bad debt	1,000
		Bal c/d	7,000
	91,000		91,000
Bal b/d	7,000		

The credit sales figure is the balancing figure. This amounts to £82,000.

Creditors

Purchases	?	Bal b/d	4,000
Bal c/d	5,000	Bank	50,000
	54,000		54,000
		Bal b/d	5,000

The balancing figure for purchases is £49,000.

Summary

Double entry bookkeeping is the means by which companies record the transactions into which they enter.

Each asset, expense, liability, income and capital balance has its own page within a ledger. Each page is called an account.

Increases in assets and expenses are recorded as debit entries in their accounts. Liabilities, income and capital are opposites in double entry terms and so increases are recorded as credits.

On a regular basis, the balances on each of the accounts are listed in a trial balance. The trial balance is then used to prepare the accounting statements.

Double entry provides an extremely effective means of calculating figures and laying out workings clearly in examinations.

2 The profit and loss account and balance sheet

The purpose of this chapter is to revise the basic steps in the preparation of the profit and loss account and balance sheet. This will lead into the preparation of statements in a form suitable for publication, a topic which will be dealt with in Chapter 3.

The chapter will commence by looking at the way in which entries in the trial balance can be rearranged to give a profit and loss account and balance sheet. The basic layout of these statements will be reviewed. The problems of accounting for fixed assets, accruals and prepayments, bad debts and proposed dividends will be considered.

Drafting these basic statements may appear to be a mechanical process. It is certainly one where a methodical approach is necessary. Having said this, it is possible to create complicated examination questions which demand a thorough understanding of the underlying concepts.

Objectives

This chapter will cover the following key issues:

- The preparation of a profit and loss account and balance sheet from a trial balance (see progress test 1)
- Accounting for fixed assets (see progress test 2)
- Adjustments for accruals and prepayments, bad debts and proposed dividends (see progress test 3)

The trial balance

The trial balance is a summary of all of the balances on the nominal ledger. It is also the basis for the preparation of the main accounting statements. A typical question will consist of a trial balance, accompanied by notes which describe a number of adjustments which have not yet been recorded in the accounts. This information must then be presented in the form of a profit and loss account and balance sheet.

Illustration 1

The following trial balance was extracted from the books of ABC Ltd, a wholesaler, at 31 December 19X3:

	Debit £000	Credit £000
Land and Buildings (cost)	610	
Plant and Machinery (cost)	430	
Fixtures and Fittings (cost)	195	
Provision for Depreciation		
Land and Buildings		15
Plant and Machinery		210
Fixtures and Fittings		75
Sales		1,480
Stock at 31 December 19X2	340	
Purchases	970	
Share Capital		625
Debenture Loans		150
Profit and Loss Account		
at 31 December 19X2		860
Debtors	355	
Creditors		215
Bank	88	
Debenture Interest	7	
Administrative Expenses	325	
Distribution Costs	185	
Investments	150	
Dividend Income		10
Rent Income		90
Dividends Paid	75	
	3,730	3,730

1. Stocks were physically counted at 31 December 19X3 and valued at £420,000.

2. The investments are to be treated as current assets.

This is a typical trial balance. The left hand column gives the debit balances, while the credit balances appear on the right. The total at the bottom of the columns has no significance whatsoever; it is simply an arithmetical check to ensure that proper double entry principles have been adhered to.

In practice, all of the final adjustments would be made by journal entry and a new trial balance prepared as a basis for the financial statements. This is unlikely to be the case in an examination question, where several adjustments are often listed in the notes to the trial balance.

The profit and loss account

The profit and loss account is used to draw all of the balances and adjustments involving income and expenses together in order to calculate the profit for the year. The statement is, in fact, an account and forms part of the double entry process. This means, for example, that the credit balance on the sales account in Illustration 1 will be transferred into the profit and loss account by the following journal:

Debit Sales   £1,480,000
  Credit Profit and Loss   £1,480,000

Thus, all of the accounts in the nominal ledger which involve income or expenses will be left with zero balances at the end of each year, ready to record the transactions of the incoming period.

Strictly speaking, the profit and loss account is not one statement but three. It comprises: (a) the trading account, which is used to calculate the difference between trading income and the direct trading costs; (b) the profit and loss account, which is used to adjust the trading profit for non-trading income and expenses; and (c) the appropriation account, which is used to show how the profit figure is either disbursed in payments of tax and dividend or retained within the company. The correct title for the statement is, therefore, the Trading and Profit and Loss and Appropriation Account. It would, however, be considered rather pedantic to write this out in full.

Gross and Net Profit

As was suggested in the previous paragraph, profit is calculated in two stages. The first figure to be derived is the trading or 'gross' profit. Gross profit is calculated by taking the income from the company's principal trading activities and subtracting the costs directly associated with earning this income. Net profit equals gross profit plus non-trading income minus non-trading expenses.

A manufacturing company's trading income, for example, would consist of the amounts obtained from the sale of the goods which it had made. Any income earned from some activity which was peripheral to the main business activities would not be treated as trading income. This would, for example, exclude the income from rents and dividends received from the calculation of trading income in Illustration 1.

The costs of generating trading income are restricted to the direct costs of purchasing or creating the goods or services which have been sold. Thus, the cost of materials bought in to be converted or resold would be treated as trading expenses, as would the cost of wages paid to production staff. Any manufacturing overhead costs would also be included in this cost. Administration, distribution and finance costs are not, however, directly related to the trading activities and should not be included in the calculation of gross profit.

There is a problem associated with accounting for the cost of materials or finished goods used or sold during the year. These are bought in by the company at their cost price and then resold at a higher selling price. This makes it extremely difficult to keep track of the asset of stock using conventional double entry techniques. This problem is overcome by having two main accounts for stock. The purchases account is used to record increases in stock, valued at cost price. The sales account is used to record decreases in stock, valued at selling price. At the end of every accounting period, the company conducts a physical stock count. The cost of stock consumed during the period is arrived at as follows:

Stock at beginning of year (from last year's stock count)

+	Purchases
−	Stock at end of year
=	Stock consumed during year

This means that the cost of stock consumed by ABC Ltd during the year ended 31 December 19X3 was:

	£000
Opening Stock	340
Purchases	970
	1,310
Closing Stock	(420)
Cost of stock consumed	890

Illustration 2

Prepare a profit and loss account for ABC Ltd for the year ended 31 December 19X3.

ABC Ltd Profit and Loss Account for the Year Ended 31 December 19X3

	£000	£000
Sales		1,480
Cost of Sales		890
Gross Profit		590
Rental Income		90
Dividend Income		10
		690
Administrative Expenses	325	
Distribution Costs	185	
		510
		180
Debenture Interest Paid		7
Net Profit		173
Dividend Paid		75
Retained Profits for Year		98
Retained Profits brought forward		860
Retained Profits carried forward		958

Notice that the statement has been given a fairly detailed heading. In practice, it is important that the statement can be identified easily, particularly by a non-accountant. It is important that the title includes the name of the company, the type of statement (e.g. a profit and loss account or balance sheet), and the date or period to which it relates.

The only trading income came from the sale of goods, the income from rents and dividends being peripheral to the main business activity. In this case, the only trading expense was the cost of goods consumed during the year. There could, however, be several items included in the cost of sales. If, for example, the company had had to convert or modify the goods before they could be sold, the labour costs associated with this modification would have to be included in the cost of sales.

It is important to ensure that the statement is as clear and as easy to understand as possible. It helps, for example, to summarise the expenses and give only sub-totals in the profit and loss account itself. This is why the detailed cost of sales workings have not been shown on the face of the statement. If the trial balance had given a more detailed breakdown of the other expenses it would still have been helpful to show only the totals for administrative and distribution costs. An analysis of these figures could have been given in a note to the statement if further details had been required.

Appropriations of Profit

The net profit of £173,000 could have been applied in three different ways. Part of the profit could have been paid out in taxes, part paid to the shareholders in dividends, and the remainder retained within the company in order to finance growth. In this case, no tax was due to be paid. A dividend payment of £75,000 was made. Retained profits for the year were £98,000. This amount was added to the retained profits brought forward from previous years to give the total amount which has been retained since the company's incorporation.

The balance sheet

The balance sheet is not an account. It is simply a list of the assets, liability and capital balances as at a point in time.

Illustration 3

Prepare a balance sheet for ABC Ltd.

ABC Ltd Balance Sheet as at 31 December 19X3

	£000	£000
Fixed Assets (see note 1)		935
Current Assets		
Stock	420	
Debtors	355	
Investments	150	
Bank	88	
	1,013	
Current Liabilities		
Creditors	215	
Net Current Assets		798
		1,733

	£000	£000
Long Term Liabilities		
Debenture Loans		150
		1,583
Capital		
Share Capital		625
Profit and Loss Account		958
		1,583

Note 1 – Fixed Assets

	Cost £000	Aggregate Depreciation £000	Net Book Value £000
Land and Buildings	610	15	595
Plant and Machinery	430	210	220
Fixtures and Fittings	195	75	120
	1,235	300	935

Notice that the first half of the balance sheet details the assets and liabilities of the company, while the second half describes the owners' capital. The two halves balance because, according to the balance sheet equation, $A - L = C$.

Fixed and Current Assets

There are two main categories of asset: fixed and current. The distinction between these has little to do with the nature of the assets themselves; it has much more to do with the motive for acquiring them.

A fixed asset is one which is intended to be retained for a relatively long time and used by the business. This would include buildings, manufacturing plant, and so on.

Notice that two balances are recorded in respect of each type of asset. Separate accounts are maintained to keep track of both the original cost of each type of asset and the amount written off to date. We shall return to the recording of fixed assets in a later section of this chapter.

A current asset is one which will be sold, consumed or converted into cash by the business in the normal course of operations. This would include stocks, amounts owed by debtors and even prepaid expenses.

An asset which would be classified as fixed by one business could be treated as current by another. Most businesses would treat vehicles, for example, as fixed assets. A vehicle distributor could, however, have bought a number of vehicles with the intention of reselling them and so they would be shown as current assets in his balance sheet.

The order in which the various assets are shown is not accidental. By convention, the assets which are most permanent or most difficult to convert into cash are shown first. Thus, premises are shown before equipment. Stock is shown first amongst the current assets because converting it into cash would involve finding a buyer, who would probably insist on a period of credit before making payment.

Current and Long Term Liabilities

A current liability is one which has to be settled within a short period of time. Balances due to be settled within 12 months are usually classified as current. Any liability which is not due to be settled within 12 months will be classified as long term.

The original term of the balance is irrelevant when classifying liabilities. If the business had taken out a 20-year loan which was due for repayment within the next year then it should be treated as a current liability.

Current liabilities are deducted from current assets to show net current assets. This is because the current assets will be used to settle these liabilities. If the business does not have sufficient current assets then it will be forced to raise additional finance or dispose of some fixed assets. It is important that management is forewarned of any possible cash shortage in plenty of time so that they can take action to remedy it.

Capital

A limited company can raise capital in two main ways: by selling shares and by creating wealth.

There are three main items which appear under the heading of share capital:

- *Ordinary share capital* is subscribed for by shareholders who then become liable to all of the risks and rewards associated with the ownership of the company.
- *Preference share capital* is purchased by shareholders who do not suffer quite the same exposure to risk as the ordinary shareholders, but who do not enjoy the same potential for profit. Typically, the preference shareholders receive a fixed annual dividend which is based on a percentage of the nominal value of their shares.

- *Share premium* is an amount paid by the shareholders in excess of the nominal value of their shares. The real worth of a company's shares is related to the dividends which are expected to be paid in the future, which is unrelated to the shares' face value. A company could, therefore, sell shares with a nominal value of 50 pence for 70 pence each, thus creating a premium of 20 pence per share.

The company can also create capital on behalf of the owners. The main way in which it does this is by generating profits from its trading activities. Any surplus profit which remains after the company has made its distributions of tax and dividends is retained on the shareholders' behalf and is used to finance the company's assets. These retained profits are called 'reserves'.

Reserves can arise in other ways. Some reserves are created by the artificial process of transferring part of the balance retained in the profit and loss account to another reserve, such as a 'general reserve'. Such a transfer has no real significance, but is intended to signal the fact that the directors have no intention of distributing these reserves in dividend payments. Reserves can also be created by the revaluation of fixed assets or as a result of the procedures which must be invoked when a company buys back its own shares.

Progress Test 1

The trial balance of DEF Ltd, an importer and wholesaler of electrical products, is given below:

DEF Ltd Trial Balance as at 31 December 19X5

	Debit £000	Credit £000
Sales		250
Stock as at 31 December 19X4	18	
Purchases	85	
Income from Sub-let of Premises		20
Wages	40	
Delivery Van Running Costs	20	
Computer Rental	15	
Office Running Costs	15	
Loan Interest	5	
Dividend Paid	25	

	Debit £000	Credit £000
Profit and Loss as at 31 December 19X4		68
Land and Buildings – Cost	170	
Fixtures and Fittings – Cost	130	
Vans – Cost	100	
Depreciation – Buildings		30
– Fixtures		110
– Vans		80
Debtors	15	
Cash	1	
Creditors		12
Bank Overdraft		4
Long Term Loan		30
Share Capital		25
Share Premium		10
	639	639

1. Stock was counted at 31 December 19X5 and valued at £13,000.

2. Expenses are to be classified under the headings of Cost of Sales, Administration, Selling and Distribution, and Finance. Detailed notes showing the composition of these items should be given.

3. The cost of wages can be analysed as follows:

	£
Electricians (who convert imported appliances to operate at UK voltages)	20,000
Secretarial and Accounting Staff	10,000
Salesman's Salary	5,000
Driver of Delivery Van	5,000
	40,000

4. The computer is used for administrative purposes.

5. The depreciation charges for the year have already been calculated and included in office running costs and delivery van running costs.

Solution to Progress Test 1

DEF Ltd Profit and Loss Account for the Year Ended 31 December 19X5

	£000	£000
Sales		250
Cost of Sales (note 1)		110
Gross Profit		140
Income from Sub-let		20
		160
Administration Costs (note 2)	40	
Selling and Distribution (note 3)	30	
Interest	5	
		75
Net Profit		85
Dividend		25
Retained Profit for Year		60
Retained Profit brought forward		68
Retained Profit carried forward		128

DEF Ltd Balance Sheet as at 31 December 19X5

	£000	£000	£000
Fixed Assets (note 4)			180
Current Assets			
Stock		13	
Debtors		15	
Cash		1	
		29	
Current Liabilities			
Bank Overdraft	4		
Creditors	12		
		16	
Net Current Assets			13
			193
Long Term Liabilities			
Long Term Loan			30
			163

	£000	£000	£000
Share Capital			25
Share Premium			10
Profit and Loss Account			128
			163

Note 1 – Cost of Sales

	£000
Opening Stock	18
Purchases	85
	103
Closing Stock	13
	90
Wages	20
	110

Note 2 – Administration Costs

	£000
Salaries	10
Computer Rental	15
Office Running Costs	15
	40

Note 3 – Selling and Distribution

	£000
Salesman's Salary	5
Driver's Wages	5
Delivery Van Running Costs	20
	30

Note 4 – Fixed Assets

	Cost	Aggregate Depreciation	Net Book Value
	£000	£000	£000
Land and Buildings	170	30	140
Fixtures and Fittings	130	110	20
Delivery Van	100	80	20
	400	220	180

Accounting for fixed assets

There are a number of interesting theoretical and conceptual issues associated with accounting for fixed assets. These are, however, outside the scope of this text. The purpose of this section is to explain how double entry bookkeeping principles can be applied to the calculation of the figures which are to appear in the final accounts. This is an important topic. The published balance sheet of a limited company must disclose a great deal of detailed information in respect of fixed assets and this is often reflected in examination questions. It is also an area where students get themselves into difficulties because they do not lay their workings out in a methodical manner.

Depreciation

Accounting for fixed assets is complicated by the fact that, with the exception of land, all assets have a limited useful life. The accounting concept of matching suggests that assets must be written off over their useful lives in order to reflect the fact that they are being consumed, albeit over a number of years, in order to generate profits. This means that the company must calculate an annual 'depreciation' charge in respect of each of its fixed assets. This charge must be shown as an expense in the profit and loss account and will also be offset against the cost of the asset in the balance sheet.

In theory, it would be possible to have just one account for each asset. The original cost would be debited to the account when the asset was purchased and the depreciation would be credited, leaving the book value which is to appear in the balance sheet as the balancing figure. In practice, this would be unacceptable because the company must disclose the original cost of its assets and also the aggregate depreciation to date in its balance sheet and so there must be two accounts for each asset, one to record the cost and the other to keep track of the depreciation.

Depreciation can be calculated in a variety of ways. The most common method is to relate the charge to the passing of time. The useful life of an asset is estimated when it is acquired. The cost is then written off over this period. Sometimes, the cost will be written off in equal instalments each year ('straight line' depreciation) and sometimes a percentage of the book value will be written off each year ('reducing balance' depreciation). Examination questions should always give precise instructions as to how depreciation should be calculated and so the practical problems of arriving at the various estimates involved can be ignored.

Illustration 4

The balances on the fixed asset accounts of GHI plc were as follows at 1 January 19X5:

	Debit £000	Credit £000
Buildings – Cost	100	
Buildings – Depreciation		20
Machinery – Cost	90	
Machinery – Depreciation		30
Vehicles – Cost	110	
Vehicles – Depreciation		50

During the year to 31 December 19X5, the company paid £40,000 for new machinery.

Buildings are to be depreciated at a rate of 4% per annum, using the straight line method.

Machinery is to be written off over ten years, using the straight line method. A full year's depreciation is to be charged in the year in which a new asset is acquired.

Vehicles are to be written off at a rate of 25% using the reducing balance method.

Prepare the fixed asset note which will appear in GHI's balance sheet as at 31 December 19X5.

In answering this question, there is no need to prepare T accounts for the cost of buildings or vehicles because the balances remain unchanged at the year end. It would also be possible to arrive at the cost of machinery without the use of an account, although it is often helpful to produce one where there has been a more complicated series of transactions. The T account for the cost of machinery is as follows:

Machinery – Cost

Bal b/d	90		
Bank	40	Bal c/d	130
	130		130
Bal b/d	130		

Buildings are to be depreciated by 4% of their cost. This means that £4,000 (£100,000 × 4%) is to be written off this year. This will be reflected in the depreciation account as follows:

Buildings – Depreciation

		Bal b/d	20
Bal c/d	24	Profit and Loss	4
	$\overline{24}$		$\overline{24}$
		Bal b/d	24

The cost of machinery is to be written off over ten years. This means that 10% of the cost of the machinery must be written off each year. The question has stated that a full year's depreciation is to be charged on the new machinery, despite the fact that it has not be owned throughout the entire year and so the charge for the year is £13,000 (£130,000 × 10%).

Machinery – Depreciation

		Bal b/d	30
Bal c/d	43	Profit and Loss	13
	$\overline{43}$		$\overline{43}$
		Bal b/d	43

Vehicles are to be depreciated using the reducing balance method. This means that the depreciation charge is to be based on the book value of the assets rather than their cost. The book value at 31 December 19X5, before charging depreciation for the year, is £60,000 (£110,000 – 50,000). Thus the depreciation charge will be £15,000 (£60,000 × 25%).

Vehicles – Depreciation

		Bal b/d	50
Bal c/d	65	Profit and Loss	15
	$\overline{65}$		$\overline{65}$
		Bal b/d	65

In each case, depreciation is recorded by a debit to the profit and loss account and a credit to the depreciation account. If expenses are to be summarised in the profit and loss account, then the depreciation charges will be shown under the most relevant headings. Thus, if the buildings are used as a factory, the depreciation on them would be included in the cost of goods sold. Depreciation on an office would be an administration charge.

The note which would be attached to the balance sheet would be as follows:

	Cost	Aggregate Depreciation	Net Book Value
	£000	£000	£000
Buildings	100	24	76
Machinery	130	43	87
Vehicles	110	65	45
	340	132	208

Disposals

In essence, the problem of adjusting for the disposal of a fixed asset is a simple one. If an asset has been disposed of, then all trace of it must be removed from the company's records. This means that both the cost and the depreciation accounts must be adjusted. It is, however, extremely difficult to do this and arrive at the correct figures for the profit and loss account and balance sheet without making use of T accounts.

The first step is to calculate the difference between the value of the asset according to the books and to compare this with the proceeds of disposal. This gain or loss on disposal will be shown in the profit and loss account. This balance should not be thought of as indicative of particularly astute or inept trading by the company. The book value of the asset is based on estimates such as the useful life which was foreseen for the asset when it was acquired and any residual amount which was expected to be recovered when it was disposed of. The balance arising on disposal is really an adjustment to the aggregate depreciation which has been charged on the asset in order to correct the inevitable forecasting errors.

The simplest means of calculating the gain or loss on disposal is to open up a disposal account. The cost of the asset and the depreciation charged to date are transferred to this account. The balance on the disposal account then comprises the book value of the asset. The proceeds of disposal, if any, are then debited to bank or sundry debtors and credited to the disposal account. The balance remaining on the disposal account represents the gain (if a credit balance) or loss (if a debit) on disposal.

Illustration 5

The following balances appear on the plant accounts of JKL Ltd as at 31 December 19X6:

	Debit £000	Credit £000
Plant – Cost	500	
Plant – Depreciation		200
Disposals		6

1. Plant is to be depreciated at a rate of 20% per annum on the reducing balance basis. A full year's depreciation is charged on the year in which an asset is acquired and none in the year of disposal. The depreciation charge for 19X6 has still to be calculated.
2. During the year, an asset which had originally cost £40,000 and on which depreciation of £30,000 had been charged was sold for £6,000. No entries have been made in respect of this transaction except for the credit of the proceeds to the disposal account.

Calculate the gain or loss on disposal and the figures which should appear in respect of plant in the profit and loss account and balance sheet of JKL Ltd.

In this case, the disposal account has already been opened and all that remains is to bring in the figures for cost and depreciation.

Disposal

Plant – Cost	40	Bank	6
		Plant – Depreciation	30
		Profit and Loss (Loss)	4
	40		40

Once the entries in respect of the book value of the asset were made, there was a debit balance of £4,000. This was then transferred to the profit and loss account as a loss on disposal.

The calculation of the depreciation charge is complicated by the fact that the opening balances have to be adjusted for the disposal in order to ensure that the charge is based on the correct amounts. Again, it is better to open up T accounts for both cost and depreciation.

Plant – Cost

Bal b/d	500	Disposal	40
		Bal c/d	460
	500		500
Bal b/d	460		

Plant – Depreciation

Disposal	30	Bal b/d	200
Bal c/d	228	Profit and Loss	58*
	258		258
		Bal b/d	228

* The depreciation charge for the year is based on the closing balance on the plant at cost account of £460,000, less the balance on the depreciation account, before charging depreciation for the year, of £170,000. This leaves a book value of £290,000 which is depreciated at 20%.

Progress Test 2

NOP plc Trial Balance as at 31 December 19X4

	Debit £000	Credit £000
Factory – Cost	400	
Factory – Depreciation		22
Machinery – Cost	430	
Machinery – Depreciation		90
Disposal		13
Office Equipment – Cost	150	
Office Equipment – Depreciation		40
Delivery Vehicles – Cost	360	
Delivery Vehicles – Depreciation		133
Sales		700
Stock at 1 January 19X4	15	
Purchases	200	
Wages – Production Staff	50	
– Clerical Staff	70	
– Sales Staff	93	
Dividend Paid	50	
Debtors	60	
Bank	10	
Creditors		25
Share Capital		200
Share Premium		215
General Reserve		100
Profit and Loss		350
	1,888	1,888

1. Stock was counted at 31 December 19X4 and was valued at £20,000.

2. During the year, an asset which had cost £30,000 and had been depreciated by £10,000 was sold for £13,000. No entries had been made in respect of this sale, apart from a credit to the disposal account in respect of the proceeds.

3. Depreciation is to be calculated as follows:

Factory	2% of cost
Machinery	10% of cost
Office equipment	20% of cost
Vehicles	25% of book value

    A full year's depreciation is to be charged in the year of acquisition and none in the year of disposal.

You are required to prepare a profit and loss account and balance sheet for the year ended 31 December 19X4.

Solution to Progress Test 2

NOP plc Profit and Loss Account for the Year Ended 31 December 19X4

	£000	£000
Sales		700
Cost of Sales (note 1)		300
Gross Profit		400
Administrative Expenses (note 2)	100	
Distribution Costs (note 3)	150	
		250
Net Profit		150
Dividends		50
Retained Profit for the Year		100
Retained Profit brought forward		350
Retained Profit carried forward		450

NOP plc Balance Sheet as at 31 December 19X4

	£000	£000
Fixed Assets (note 4)		900
Current Assets		
Stock	20	
Debtors	60	
Bank	10	
	90	
Current Liabilities		
Creditors	25	
		65
		965
Share Capital		200
Share Premium		215
General Reserve		100
Profit and Loss Account		450
		965

Note 1 – Cost of Sales

	£000
Materials (working 1)	195
Wages	50
Depreciation of Factory (working 2)	8
Depreciation of Machinery (working 3)	40
Loss on Disposal of Machinery (working 3)	7
	300

Note 2 – Administrative Expenses

	£000
Salaries	70
Depreciation of Office Equipment (working 4)	30
	100

Note 3 – Distribution Costs

	£000
Salesmen's wages	93
Depreciation of Delivery Vehicles (working 5)	57
	150

Note 4 – Fixed Assets

	Cost	Aggregate Depreciation	Net Book Value
	£000	£000	£000
Factory	400	30	370
Machinery	400	120	280
Office Equipment	150	70	80
Delivery Vehicles	360	190	170
	1,310	410	900

Workings

1. Materials

	£000
Opening Stock	15
Purchases	200
Closing Stock	(20)
	195

2. Depreciation of Factory = £400,000 × 2% = £8,000
   This is added to the balance brought forward of £22,000 to give a closing balance on the depreciation account of £30,000.

3. Machinery
   The adjustments required in respect of the disposal mean that it would be wise to produce T accounts to support this figure.

Disposal

Machinery – Cost	30	Bank	13
		Machinery – Depreciation	10
		Profit and Loss (Loss)	7
	30		30

Machinery – Cost

Bal b/d	430	Disposal	30
		Bal c/d	400
	430		430
Bal b/d	400		

Machinery – Depreciation

Disposal	10	Bal b/d	90
Bal c/d	120	Profit and Loss	40*
	130		130
		Bal b/d	120

*

   The depreciation charge is based on the cost of £400,000 × 10% = £40,000

4.   Office Equipment
     Depreciation = £150,000 × 20% = £30,000
     This gives a balance carried forward on the depreciation account of
     £40,000 + £30,000 = £70,000.

5.   Vehicles
     Depreciation is to be calculated on the reducing balance basis. This
     means that the charge = (£360,000 – 133,000) × 25% = £57,000
     (rounded off to the nearest thousand).
     The balance carried forward on the depreciation account = (£133,000
     + 57,000) = £190,000.

Note that the figures in the question were expressed in thousands and so the
calculation of the depreciation charge was also rounded off to the nearest
thousand. It is always wise to work in the same units as are used in the
question. There should be no penalty for sensible rounding.

Notes versus Workings

Notes are intended for publication along with the statements themselves so
that the readers can be informed about the data which have been omitted
from the profit and loss account and balance sheet for the sake of clarity.
     Workings, on the other hand, would never be published. They are intended
to give the examiner an indication of the logic underlying an attempted
solution to a question. It is almost inevitable that minor differences of
opinion will arise over the treatment of certain items and that most solutions
will contain some errors. If all of the figures are simply produced on a
student's calculator and are not submitted then there is a very real danger
that a disproportionate number of marks will be lost for every trivial error.

Other adjustments

The depreciation adjustment may be one of the most complicated which has to be made to the figures in the trial balance, but it is by no means the only one.

Accruals and Prepayments

It may be necessary to adjust for expenses which have been incurred, but not yet invoiced (e.g. electricity consumed since the latest quarterly bill) or for payments which partly relate to the next accounting period (e.g. an annual insurance premium paid before the year end).

In practice, the necessary adjustments would be made by journal entry and the corrected figures would appear in the trial balance. This is unlikely to be the case in an examination question. Fortunately, the treatment of this type of balance is very straightforward and does not require detailed workings.

Any unrecorded expenses should be added to the relevant item in the profit and loss account. This is effectively a debit entry. The related credit is recorded by creating the liability of 'accruals' in the current liabilities section of the balance sheet. It is always a sensible precaution to show the calculation of these figures in the workings, although there is rarely any need to provide detailed T accounts.

Advance payments are dealt with in a similar manner. They are deducted from the relevant item in the profit and loss account, thereby making a credit entry. The corresponding debit takes the form of an increase in the current asset of 'prepayments' in the balance sheet.

Sometimes examiners provide information about accruals in an oblique way. The most obvious example of this is a reference in the trial balance to a loan of, say, £100,000 on which the rate of interest is 10%. If the cost of interest according to the trial balance is less than £10,000 (i.e. £100,000 × 10%) then it should be assumed that the remainder of the charge should be accrued.

Bad Debts

If a debtor's balance is unlikely to be settled then it has become worthless and should be written off by debiting the expense of bad debts and crediting the debtors account. The cost of bad debts incurred can be difficult to classify. It could be treated as a distribution cost because the company is obliged to provide credit in order to make sales and this leads to the risk of default.

When preparing the balance sheet, it is important to consider the possibility that some of the debtors will become insolvent after the year end and will be unable to pay the amounts owed to the company. In order to ensure that the cost of bad debts is recorded in full, and also to avoid the possibility that the value of debtors is overstated in the balance sheet, it is customary to create a provision for bad debts. This provision is then deducted from the gross value of debtors when drafting the balance sheet.

If the company has had a provision for bad debts in previous years then there will be an account with a credit balance brought forward from the previous year. This balance will have to be adjusted to the correct amount as at the end of the year. An increase in the provision is recorded by debiting (and therefore increasing) bad debts and crediting the provision account; a decrease is recorded by crediting bad debts and debiting the provision account.

Illustration 6

The following balances appear in respect of debtors in the trial balance of QRS Ltd as at 31 December 19X7:

	Debit £000	Credit £000
Debtors	600	
Bad Debts	10	
Provision for Bad Debts		15

The provision for bad debts is to be adjusted to 4% of debtors at the year end.

State the amounts which will appear in the profit and loss account and balance sheet in respect of debtors.

The provision at the year end will equal £24,000 (i.e. £600,000 × 4%), which means that the balance on the provision account will have to be increased by £9,000 (i.e. £24,000 – 15,000). The total cost of bad debts is £19,000 (i.e. £10,000 + 9,000).

Debtors will be valued at £576,000 in the balance sheet (i.e. £600,000 – 24,000). It is better to state this net amount in the balance sheet and to show the calculation of this figure in the workings.

Proposed Dividends

It is unusual for all of the annual dividend to be paid to shareholders during the year. Normally, an interim payment is made during the year and the directors propose a final dividend for ratification at the company's annual general meeting. The amount which is proposed by the directors should be added to the amount paid to show the total dividend for the year in the appropriation section of the profit and loss account. This debit entry will then be accompanied by a credit in the form of the current liability of proposed dividend.

Preference shares can create the possibility of another 'concealed' accrual. The holders of preference shares are usually entitled to a fixed annual rate of dividend, expressed as a percentage of the nominal value of the shares. Normally, the company would be obliged to pay the preference dividend in full. If it defaults for any reason, the directors would usually be barred from proposing to pay an ordinary dividend. Therefore, if the company has, say, £200,000 of 7% preference shares, then the dividend to these shareholders amounts to £14,000 (i.e. £200,000 × 7%). If the trial balance suggests that a lesser amount has been paid then the deficit should be treated as a proposed dividend.

Avoiding omissions

It is easy to overlook an entry in the trial balance or to make an incomplete adjustment to one or more of the notes, especially if one is working under examination conditions. It is surprising, therefore, that many students do not bother to take the simplest of precautions when preparing a solution. One useful tip is to place a tick against each figure or adjustment once it has been included in one of the statements. This means that each figure in the trial balance should have been ticked once and each of the notes twice by the time the balance sheet has been completed. Any omissions can be spotted more easily if this is done.

While it is always reassuring to discover that the balance sheet is square, it is not a guarantee that the figures in the statement are actually correct. It is never worth spending a great deal of time looking for the cause of the difference, especially when there are time constraints such as in an examination.

Progress Test 3

Using the following information, prepare a profit and loss account and balance sheet for TUV plc, a manufacturing company.

TUV plc Trial Balance as at 31 December 19X7

	Debit £000	Credit £000
Sales		1,000
Machinery – Cost	588	
Machinery – Depreciation		180
Computer – Cost	250	
Computer – Depreciation		50
Warehouse – Cost	700	
Warehouse – Depreciation		96
Delivery Vehicles – Cost	230	
Delivery Vehicles – Depreciation		80
Disposal		10
Stock at 1 January 19X7	20	
Purchases of Materials	250	
Repairs to Machinery	27	
Rent – Factory	28	
– Offices	32	
Manufacturing Wages	49	
Directors' Salaries	35	
Clerical Staff Salaries	18	
Office Heating and Lighting	9	
Sales Commission	68	
Road Tax and Insurance on Vehicles	30	
Bad Debts	50	
Provision for Bad Debts		1
Loan Interest	20	
Debtors	84	
Bank	105	
Creditors		26
10% Debenture Loans		400
Interim Ordinary Dividend	30	
8% Preference Shares		250
Ordinary Shares		310
Profit and Loss Account		220
	2,623	2,623

1. Stock was counted on 31 December 19X7 and valued at £25,000.
2. The company's auditors have discovered that the acquisition of a piece of machinery costing £12,000 has been posted incorrectly to the repairs account. No adjustment has been made in respect of this error.
3. The balance on the disposals account represents the proceeds of the disposal of a delivery vehicle which had originally cost £30,000 and which had been depreciated by £13,000. No other entries have been made in respect of this transaction.
4. Depreciation has still to be charged as follows:

Machinery	10% straight line
Computer	20% straight line
Warehouse	2% straight line
Delivery Vehicles	25% reducing balance

5. The computer is used mainly for accounting and payroll purposes.
6. The following expenses have been incurred but not recorded:

	£000
Manufacturing Wages	1
Factory Rent	2
Clerical Salaries	2
Office Heating	4

   The company paid £10,000 during the year in order to insure the delivery vehicles for the 12-month period from 1 July 19X7 to 30 June 19X8.
7. The provision for bad debts has to be increased to £4,000.
8. The directors propose to pay the preference dividend in full and to make a final ordinary dividend payment of £50,000.

Solution to Progress Test 3

TUV plc Profit and Loss Account for the Year Ended 31 December 19X7

	£000	£000
Sales		1,000
Cost of Goods Sold (note 1)		400
Gross Profit		600
Administration Costs (note 2)	150	
Distribution Costs (note 3)	200	

	£000	£000
		350
		250
Interest		40
Net Profit		210
Dividends (note 4)		100
Retained Profit for the Year		110
Retained Profit brought forward		220
Retained Profit carried forward		330

TUV plc Balance Sheet as at 31 December 19X7

	£000	£000	£000
Fixed Assets (note 5)			1,200
Current Assets			
Stock		25	
Debtors		80	
Prepaid Expenses		5	
Bank		105	
		215	
Current Liabilities			
Creditors	26		
Accrued Expenses	29		
Proposed Dividend	70		
		125	
Net Current Assets			90
			1,290
Long Term Liabilities			
10% Debenture Loan			400
			890
Ordinary Share Capital			310
Preference Share Capital			250
Profit and Loss Account			330
			890

Note 1 – Cost of Goods Sold

	£000
Materials	245
Wages	50
Rent	30
Machinery Repairs	15
Machinery Depreciation	60
	400

Note 2 – Administration Costs

	£000
Directors' Salaries	35
Clerical Wages	20
Office Heating and Lighting	13
Computer Depreciation	50
Office Rent	32
	150

Note 3 – Distribution Costs

	£000
Sales Commission	68
Road Tax and Insurance	25
Bad Debts	53
Vehicle Depreciation	33
Loss on Disposal of Vehicle	7
Warehouse Depreciation	14
	200

Note 4 – Dividends

	Paid	Proposed	Total
	£000	£000	£000
Ordinary	30	50	80
Preference	–	20	20
	30	70	100

Note 5 – Fixed Assets

	Cost	Aggregate Depreciation	Net Book Value
	£000	£000	£000
Warehouse	700	110	590
Machinery	600	240	360
Computer	250	100	150
Vehicles	200	100	100
	1,750	550	1,200

Workings

1. Loan Interest
   £400,000 × 10% = £40,000 (of which £20,000 is accrued)

2. Accrued Expenses
   The charges referred to in note 6 of the question have been added to their respective expenses. These have led to a liability of £9,000, to which must be added the £20,000 accrued interest to give a total liability for accruals of £29,000.

3. Machinery
   The expense of repairs has had to be reduced by £12,000 to £15,000 and the cost of machinery increased by this amount to £600,000.
   Depreciation on machinery = £600,000 × 10% = £60,000

4. Debtors
   Bad debts written off amount to £50,000, to which must be added the increase in the provision of £3,000 to give a total cost for bad debts of £53,000.
   The gross value of debtors is £84,000. This is adjusted by deducting the provision for bad debts of £4,000 to leave the net value of £80,000.

5. Vehicles

	Disposal		
Cost	30	Bank	10
		Depreciation	13
		Profit and Loss	7
	30		30

The cost of vehicles is reduced to £200,000 and the value of depreciation brought forward to £67,000. This means that the depreciation charge = (£200,000 – 67,000) × 25% = £33,000 (rounded).

Summary

The profit and loss account and balance sheet are intended to inform their readers about a company's performance and financial position. The preparation of these statements is frequently tested in the examinations of all of the professional accounting bodies.

It is important to adopt a methodical approach to these questions. There is often a great deal of material to be processed under severe time pressure.

The statements should be made as clear as possible by relegating some of the detailed figures to notes which should be cross-referenced to their related sub-totals.

Detailed workings should be submitted on a separate sheet. These would not be published in practice, but are a vital aid to the examiner who wishes to see the logic underlying the answer.

3 Published accounts

Every limited company must publish an annual report. This should include a profit and loss account, a balance sheet and a set of supporting notes. A copy must be sent to every shareholder and another must be filed with the Registrar of Companies, where it will be held for inspection by other interested parties. This is a legal requirement which is intended to protect the company's shareholders by ensuring that they, or their professional advisers, have sufficient information upon which to base important decisions about the retention of their shares, the re-election of directors, and so on.

The responsibility for the preparation of the annual report lies with the directors. Unfortunately, this creates certain conflicts of interest. The directors may wish to manipulate the results in order to create the impression that the company is better managed than it actually is. They will also be reluctant to publish any information which could be of commercial value to a competitor. Thus, the preparation of the statements must be regulated in order to ensure that the figures which are published are both reliable and comprehensive.

This chapter will commence with an overview of the regulations which affect published accounts. This will be followed by a description of the formats which must be used for the presentation of the profit and loss account and balance sheet. The additional disclosures which must be made will be illustrated by looking at four of the main notes which must be attached to the statements. Finally, the disclosure of accounting policies will be considered.

Objectives

This chapter covers the following key objectives:

- The preparation of the profit and loss account and balance sheet in the formats specified by the Companies Act 1985 (see progress test 1)
- The preparation of the more common notes to the financial statements (see progress tests 2 and 3)

Regulations affecting the preparation of published accounts

In broad terms, there are three main bodies of rules which affect the preparation of financial statements:

(i)   Company law

The Companies Act 1985 prescribes formats for the presentation of the profit and loss account and the balance sheet and also contains most of the detailed disclosure requirements. The Act also imposes a requirement that the statements must give a 'true and fair view' of the company's profitability and financial position. The concept of truth and fairness is not defined. Its application could, for example, mean that the company must disclose more than the information specifically required by the Companies Act if further disclosure is necessary in order to provide an understanding of the company's performance or position. (You may be aware that there are actually two Companies Acts, the Companies Act 1985 and the Companies Act 1989. Virtually all of the accounting provisions of the Companies Act 1989 consist of modifications to the Companies Act 1985. Thus, all references will be to the Companies Act 1985—updated as necessary for the changes in the 1989 Act—unless it is stated otherwise.)

*(ii)   Financial Reporting Standards and Statements of Standard Accounting
        Practice*

The flexibility inherent in accounting for a variety of contentious items led to a crisis of confidence in the accountancy profession. The profession reacted by initiating a programme of standard setting designed to reduce the number of permissible treatments of certain transactions and balances. At the time of writing, the following of these 'Statements of Standard Accounting Practice' (SSAPs) and 'Financial Reporting Standards' (FRSs) are in force:

1   Accounting for Associated Companies (1982)
2   Disclosure of Accounting Policies (1971)
3   Earnings per Share (1974)
4   The Accounting Treatment of Government Grants (1974)
5   Accounting for Value Added Tax (1974)
6   Extraordinary Items and Prior Year Adjustments (1986)
8   The Treatment of Taxation under the Imputation System in the
    Accounts of Companies (1974)
9   Stocks and Long Term Contracts (1988)
12 Accounting for Depreciation (1987)
13 Accounting for Research and Development (1989)
14 Group Accounts (1978)

15   Accounting for Deferred Tax (1985)
17   Accounting for Post Balance Sheet Events (1980)
18   Accounting for Contingencies (1980)
19   Accounting for Investment Properties (1981)
20   Foreign Currency Translation (1983)
21   Accounting for Leases and Hire Purchase Contracts (1984)
22   Accounting for Goodwill (1984)
23   Accounting for Acquisitions and Mergers (1985)
24   Accounting for Pension Costs (1988)
25   Segmental Reporting (1990)
FRS1 Cash Flow Statements (1991)

The dates in brackets refer to the years in which the standards were issued. There are breaks in the numerical sequence because SSAPs 7, 10, 11 and 16 have been withdrawn and not replaced. The list does not appear to be in chronological order because a number of SSAPs have been withdrawn and replaced with revised statements which have the same numbers.

In 1990, the Accounting Standards Committee was replaced by a new body, the Accounting Standards Board (ASB). This was more than a change of name. The ASB has the power to issue accounting standards (known as 'Financial Reporting Standards' or FRSs) under its own authority. The ASC's efforts were sometimes hampered by the fact that it had to obtain the backing of the Councils of each of the professional accounting bodies for any new standards. The ASB will also have additional resources made available to it. An independent body, the Financial Reporting Council, has been created to oversee the ASB and to raise funds on its behalf.

The setting up of the ASB has not made the SSAPs redundant. Indeed, the ASB has adopted the standards which were in force at the time of its creation.

Company law and accounting standards tend to complement each other, in that the former concentrates on listing the information which is to be published, while the latter state how these figures are to be calculated.

(iii) Stock Exchange requirements
Those companies which are listed on the Stock Exchange are required to publish a few pieces of additional information, notably certain analyses of profit and details of shareholdings.

The preparation of accounting statements which comply with these requirements and are, therefore, 'in a form suitable for publication' is more than a common source of examination questions. At intermediate and advanced levels, these statements can form the basis of entire papers. The purpose of this chapter is to develop a methodology which can be used to learn and apply these rules.

Learning the Disclosure Requirements

The sheer quantity of information which must be published can be gauged by the fact that shareholders are often provided with annual reports which exceed 50 pages in length. Even though half of this may be material of a promotional nature or consist of other voluntary disclosures, the annual report is a detailed document. While examination questions cannot, of course, contain this amount of material, a typical solution could be seven or eight pages long and be expected to take an hour or more to complete.

The published accounts of real companies are a useful learning and revision aid. These are not difficult to obtain. Many companies, especially the larger ones, advertise the availability of their annual reports in the business pages of the quality press and are happy to send a copy to anyone who requests one. Alternatively, a polite letter addressed to the company secretary or financial director and posted to the head office of almost any large company will often prove fruitful. It is easy to build up a small collection of, say, between six and ten annual reports. This collection should concentrate on manufacturing and retailing companies and avoid the financial institutions, which are subject to different regulations. Reading these statements thoroughly will also show how figures can be laid out neatly and concisely.

A detailed description of the publication requirements would be outside the scope of this book. Instead, it is intended to illustrate them by looking at the prescribed formats for the main statements and also at four of the main notes which must be published in support of them.

Statutory formats

The Companies Act requires that both the profit and loss account and the balance sheet should be laid out in accordance with approved formats. There are four acceptable formats for the profit and loss account and two for the balance sheet. In practice, the choice tends to be between only two of the formats for the profit statement because the other two are broadly similar, but have been rearranged in a rather old-fashioned 'two-sided' manner. For the same reason, only one of the balance sheet formats is used.

It is permissible to modify the formats to quite a large extent. Many of the headings in the profit and loss account and many of the sub-headings in the balance sheet can be combined, provided that there is a suitable analysis in the notes to the statements. It is also possible to add additional headings and sub-headings as long as they are consistent with the other items in the formats. This flexibility is intended to make the statements themselves easier for the shareholders to read, but it also simplifies the task of the student who would otherwise have much more to remember.

The Profit and Loss Account Formats

The two formats which are commonly used are described by the Companies Act as 'Format 1' and 'Format 2'. Format 1 classifies expenses by function (i.e. cost of goods sold, distribution cost, etc.), while Format 2 classifies by type of expense (i.e. cost of materials, staff costs, depreciation, etc.). Most companies opt for Format 1 and this is reflected by the fact that a large proportion of examination questions would appear to have been written so that this format is easier to apply.

The following are 'abridged' versions of the formats. They have been derived from the Companies Act itself, but have been modified by the exclusion of certain lines which are almost certain to be irrelevant and by a certain amount of permissible combination of headings.

Illustration 1 – Profit and Loss Account Formats

Format 1 – Expenses classified by function

	£	£	
Turnover		x	
Cost of Sales		(x)	
Gross Profit		x	
Distribution Costs	(x)		
Administrative Expenses	(x)		
Other Operating Income	x		
		(x)	
Operating Profit		x	*1
Income from Investments	x		*2
Interest Receivable	x		
Interest Payable	(x)		
		(x)	
Profit on Ordinary Activities		x	
Tax on Profit on Ordinary Activities		(x)	
Profit on Ordinary Activities after Taxation		x	
Extraordinary Items		(x)	
Profit for the Financial Year		x	*3
Dividends		(x)	
Profit Retained for the Year		x	

See notes overleaf

Retained Profits brought forward		x
Retained Profits carried forward		x

Format 2 – Expenses classified by type

	£	£	
Turnover		x	
Operating Expenses		(x)	*4
Operating Profit		x	
Income from Investments	x		
Interest Receivable	x		
Interest Payable	(x)		
		(x)	
Profit on Ordinary Activities		x	
Tax on Profit on Ordinary Activities		(x)	
Profit on Ordinary Activities after Taxation		x	
Extraordinary Items		(x)	
Profit for the Financial Year		x	*3
Dividends		(x)	
Profit Retained for the Year		x	
Retained Profits brought forward		x	
Retained Profits carried forward		x	

*1   There is no official title for this sub-heading. It is, however, convenient to attach a label to it.

*2   There are several categories of investment income, although it is unlikely that any of the sub-headings will be relevant to most examination questions.

*3   The formats do not require an appropriation section as such although, again, it is convenient to provide one.

*4   Under Format 2, Operating Expenses have to be analysed to show the amounts of:

	£
Change in Stock of Finished Goods and Work-in-Progress	(x)
Other Operating Income	x
Raw Materials and Consumables	(x)
Other External Charges	(x)
Staff Costs	(x)
Depreciation	(x)
Other Operating Charges	(x)
	(x)

There is no need to show nil entries in respect of irrelevant headings.

There are no statutory definitions of the various headings within the formats and there are legitimate differences of opinion about where certain items should be included. It is important, therefore, to submit a clear set of workings so that the examiner can see how each figure has been arrived at.

Illustration 2 – Balance Sheet Format

	£	£	
Fixed Assets			
Intangible Assets		x	
Tangible Assets		x	*1
Investments		x	
		x	
Current Assets			
Stocks	x		*2
Debtors	x		
Investments	x		
Cash at Bank	x		
	x		
Creditors: Amounts falling due			
within one year	(x)		*3
Net Current Assets		x	
Total Assets less Current Liabilities		x	
Creditors: Amounts falling due			
after more than one year		(x)	*3
Provisions for Liabilities and Charges		(x)	
		x	
Capital and Reserves			
Called-up Share Capital		x	
Share Premium Account		x	
Revaluation Reserve		x	
Other Reserves		x	
Profit and Loss Account		x	
		x	

*1   Tangible fixed assets must be broken down as follows:

	£
Land and Buildings	x
Plant and Machinery	x
Fixtures, Fittings, Tools and Equipment	x
Payments on account and assets in the course of construction	x
	$\overline{x}$

It is permissible to provide more detail than the Act requires. If the question gives figures for, say, vehicles these could either be added to the total for plant and machinery or shown separately in the fixed assets note. The latter course of action is usually quicker and equally correct.

*2 Stocks must be broken down as follows:

	£
Raw Materials and Consumables	x
Work-in-Progress	x
Finished Goods and Goods for Sale	x
Payments on Account	x
	$\overline{x}$

*3 These headings for current and long term liabilities are rather cumbersome. They are, however, required by the Act. Each of these totals must be broken down as follows:

	£
Debenture Loans	x
Bank Loans and Overdrafts	x
Payments Received on Account	x
Trade Creditors	x
Bills of Exchange Payable	x
Other Creditors Including Taxation and Social Security	x
Accruals and Deferred Income	x
	$\overline{x}$

It may be unnecessary to relegate this detailed analysis to supporting notes. If only a few of the sub-headings are relevant then it is perfectly acceptable to show all of the figures on the face of the balance sheet itself.

It is inefficient and unproductive to attempt to memorise the formats by rote learning. It is much more effective to develop familiarity with them by practising on as many questions as possible, either from textbooks or past examination papers. Three questions are provided for this purpose in this chapter and others in the one which follows.

Progress Test 1

Use the following information to prepare two profit and loss accounts (using each of Formats 1 and 2) and a balance sheet for BCD plc. These should be in a form suitable for publication.

BCD plc Trial Balance as at 31 December 19X7

	£000	£000
Wages	868	
Rates	54	
Electricity	144	
Spare Parts and Lubricants (for plant and machinery)	46	
Vehicle Running Costs	30	
Sales Commission	90	
Bank		70
Creditors		313
Debtors	412	
15% Debentures		200
Debenture Interest	15	
Buildings – Cost	300	
Buildings – Depreciation		60
Plant and Machinery – Cost	560	
Plant and Machinery – Depreciation		140
Vehicles – Cost	350	
Vehicles – Depreciation		170
Purchase of Materials	287	
Sales		1,900
Stocks – Raw Materials	70	
– Work-in-Progress	130	
– Finished Goods	60	
Share Capital		300
Share Premium		100
Profit and Loss Account		163
	3,416	3,416

1.   Wages can be analysed as follows:

	£000
Manufacturing Staff	620
Clerical and Management Staff	180
Warehouse Staff	68
	868

2. Rates are to be apportioned between the factory, the administrative offices and the warehouse in the ratio 6:2:1 and electricity in the ratio 4:1:1.
3. Stocks were physically counted at 31 December 19X7 and were valued as follows:

	£000
Raw Materials	90
Work-in-Progress	140
Finished Goods	70
	300

4. Depreciation is to be charged as follows:

Buildings	2% straight line (4:1:1 to factory, offices and warehouse)
Plant and machinery	20% reducing balance
Vehicles	25% reducing balance

5. The figure for vehicle running expenses includes £7,000 which has been prepaid.
6. Provision has to be made for £5,000 of sales commission which has been incurred but not yet recorded and also for the unpaid debenture interest.
7. The directors propose to pay an ordinary dividend of £20,000.

Solution to Progress Test 1

BCD plc Profit and Loss Account for the Year Ended 31 December 19X7 (Format 1)

	£000	£000
Turnover		1,900
Cost of Sales		(1,133)
Gross Profit		767
Distribution Costs	(262)	
Administrative Expenses	(217)	
		(479)
Operating Profit		288
Interest Payable		(30)
Profit for the Financial Year		258
Dividends		(20)
Profit Retained for the Year		238
Retained Profits brought forward		163
Retained Profits carried forward		401

BCD plc Profit and Loss Account for the Year Ended 31 December 19X7 (Format 2)

	Notes	£000
Turnover		1,900
Operating Expenses	[1]	(1,612)
Operating Profit		288
Interest Payable		(30)
Profit for the Financial Year		258
Dividends		(20)
Profit Retained for the Year		238
Retained Profits brought forward		163
Retained Profits carried forward		401

BCD plc Balance Sheet as at 31 December 19X7

	Notes	£000	£000	£000
Fixed Assets				
Tangible Assets	[2]			705
Current Assets				
Stocks	[3]		300	
Debtors			419	
			719	
Creditors: Amounts falling due within one year				
Bank Overdraft		(70)		
Creditors		(353)		
			(423)	
Net Current Assets				296
Total Assets less Current Liabilities				1,001
Creditors: Amounts falling due after more than one year				
Debentures				(200)
				801
Capital and Reserves				
Called-up Share Capital				300
Share Premium Account				100
Profit and Loss Account				401
				801

Note 1 – Operating Expenses (Format 2 only)

	£000
Change in Stock of Finished	
Goods and Work-in-Progress	20
Raw Materials and Consumables	(313)
Other External Charges	(221)
Staff Costs	(963)
Depreciation	(135)
	(1,612)

Note 2 – Tangible Fixed Assets

	Cost	Aggregate Depreciation	Net Book Value
	£000	£000	£000
Buildings	300	66	234
Plant and Machinery	560	224	336
Vehicles	350	215	135
	1,210	505	705

Note 3 – Stock

	£000
Raw Materials	90
Work-in-Progress	140
Finished Goods	70
	300

Workings

Raw Materials and Consumables

	£000
Opening Stock	70
Purchases	287
Closing Stock	(90)
	267
Spare Parts and Lubricants	46
	313

Cost of Sales (Format 1)

	£000
Raw Materials and Consumables	313
Increase in Work-in-Progress and Finished Goods	(20)
Manufacturing Wages	620
Factory Rates ($54 \times \frac{6}{9}$)	36
Factory Electricity ($144 \times \frac{4}{6}$)	96
Depreciation – Factory ($6 \times \frac{4}{6}$)	4
– Plant	84
	1,133

Distribution Costs (Format 1)

	£000
Wages	68
Rates ($54 \times \frac{1}{9}$)	6
Electricity ($144 \times \frac{1}{6}$)	24
Vehicle Running ($30 - 7$)	23
Commission ($90 + 5$)	95
Warehouse Depreciation ($6 \times \frac{1}{6}$)	1
Vehicle Depreciation	45
	262

Administrative Expenses (Format 1)

	£000
Salaries	180
Rates ($54 \times \frac{2}{9}$)	12
Electricity ($144 \times \frac{1}{6}$)	24
Office Depreciation ($6 \times \frac{1}{6}$)	1
	217

Other External Charges (Format 2)

	£000
Rates	54
Electricity	144
Vehicle Running Costs	23
	221

Depreciation

	£000
Buildings ($300 \times 2\%$)	6
Plant and Machinery ($420 \times 20\%$)	84
Vehicles ($180 \times 25\%$)	45
	135

It is unlikely that an examination question will require the preparation of two profit statements. It is much more likely that the question will either state which of the two formats is to be adopted or will leave the choice of format to the candidate. The examiner may express a preference for one of the two formats by analysing the expenses in the trial balance in such a way that one format would be much easier to produce than the other.

Notes to the accounts

The profit and loss account and balance sheet rarely exceed one page each. Most of the detailed information in a company's annual report is provided in the notes which accompany the main statements. It has already been shown that notes can be a useful means of reducing the amount of data included in the statements themselves. They are also used to disclose facts and figures which are required specifically by the Companies Act or by one of the accounting standards.

This section will describe four of the main notes which are published in the annual report. These four have been selected because they tend to appear regularly in examination questions. There is, of course, no guarantee that each of these notes will be part of the solution to any given question and it is also possible that some of the other disclosure requirements, which are not discussed in this book, will be examined.

It has already been suggested that it is important to lay solutions out in a manner which is easy to read. Many students' scripts are difficult to follow because statements, notes and workings become jumbled together. This can be prevented by heading up several sheets of paper before starting to answer the question itself. The profit and loss account and balance sheet will require one sheet each, the notes at least two and the workings at least one. Doing this will encourage a much more orderly approach to the question, which will lead to a neater script and will also save time.

Operating Expenses

The Companies Act and, to a lesser extent, some of the accounting standards assume that the shareholders must be told how much has been spent on certain expenses. Typically, these expenses are presented as a list in a note which supports the figure for the operating profit.

Depreciation

The total amount of depreciation should be stated (unless, of course, it has already been stated because profit and loss account Format 2 has been used).

The shareholders require this figure so that they can recalculate it using a different method. This will enable them to compare the company's results with those of another which has a different depreciation policy.

Directors' emoluments

The total amount should be stated, including the value of any pension contributions paid on the directors' behalf.

The shareholders will have an obvious interest in the amount which the directors are paying to themselves. In fact, there is usually a further note which is devoted to the analysis of this amount.

Employees

The total remuneration paid to employees (including directors) has to be stated. This has to be broken down to show the amounts paid for wages and salaries, social security costs and pension costs. It is also necessary to state the average weekly number of employees, which must be analysed into 'appropriate' categories.

Hire charges

If material amounts are paid for the hire of plant and machinery or other assets then these amounts must be stated.

By hiring assets, rather than purchasing them outright, the company is effectively obtaining the benefits of ownership without any corresponding assets or liabilities appearing in the balance sheet. This can have the effect of making the company appear to be more efficient than it actually is. The requirement to disclose hire charges is one way in which this anomaly can be dealt with.

Auditor's remuneration

The auditor's remuneration, including any expenses related to the audit, must be disclosed.

This is one means by which the shareholders can assess the extent to which the auditor can be manipulated by the directors. An excessive fee is tantamount to a bribe, while an inadequate fee would imply that the directors have managed to pressurise the auditor into conducting a superficial inquiry.

There is currently no requirement to disclose any amounts paid to the auditor in respect of any other services which he or she provides. Thus, any amounts which are paid in respect of, say, tax advice should be disregarded. This could, however, change because the Companies Act 1989 modified the Companies Act 1985 to give the Secretary of State the power to require further disclosures of amounts paid to auditors.

Research and development

SSAP 13 requires public and some private companies to disclose the amount spent during the year on research and development. This should be split between current expenditure and amounts amortised from deferred expenditure.

Directors' Remuneration

The legislation regarding directors' remuneration is extremely complex. Fortunately, some of the problems which are faced by accountants in practice are impossible to replicate under examination conditions. For example, the total for remuneration should include the value of benefits in kind, such as company cars, private health insurance and so on. The value of these benefits can be arrived at in a number of different ways, although a question would have to state clearly how they should be measured.

The payment of pension contributions can prove confusing. The amount which appears in the note for operating profits and the first analysis which appears in the note dealing with directors' emoluments should both include pension contributions. Any amounts appearing thereafter should exclude this cost.

Part of the remuneration paid to an executive director will be in respect of his or her duties as a member of the board, such as attending board meetings, while the remainder will be paid in respect of the managerial aspect of the job. Some directors have no direct managerial responsibilities. The amounts paid to these non-executive directors are entirely in respect of their membership of the board. Total remuneration, including any pension contributions, must be broken down to show how much has been paid as 'directors' fees' and how much as 'other emoluments'.

The note must also disclose the amount paid to each individual director. This is done by stating the total amount, this time excluding pension contributions, paid to the chair of the board. The amount paid to the highest-paid director, again excluding pension contributions, must also be stated (unless the chair is the highest paid). There is no need to state the actual amounts paid to the remaining directors, although the numbers of directors whose emoluments fall within bands of £5,000, yet again excluding pension contributions, must be stated.

Illustration 3

The emoluments paid to the directors of DEF plc during the year ended 31 December 19X6 were as follows:

	Fees	Salaries	Pension Contributions
	£000	£000	£000
Mr Black (Chairman)	7	30	4
Mr Brown (Managing)	8	32	3
Mrs Red (Personnel)	3	20	3
Mr Orange (Finance)	4	22	3
Mrs Yellow (non-executive)	6	–	–
Mr Green (non-executive)	4	–	–
	32	104	13

Total emoluments, including pension contributions, are £149,000.

Mr Brown is the highest-paid director (£40,000, excluding pension contributions).

The directors' emoluments note in DEF's annual report would appear as follows:

Directors' emoluments

	£000
Fees	32
Other emoluments	117
	149

The emoluments of the chairman, excluding pension contributions, were

£37,000. The emoluments of the highest-paid director, excluding pension contributions, were £40,000.

The emoluments, excluding pension contributions, of the other directors fell within the following ranges:

£	
0 – 5,000	1
5,001 – 10,000	1
20,001 – 25,000	1
25,001 – 30,000	1

Extraordinary Items

The Companies Act formats make provision for extraordinary items to be highlighted on the face of the profit and loss account. These items are defined by SSAP 6. If an extraordinary event has had a drastic effect on the company's results, then the operating profit should be calculated as if this event had not occurred, thus giving the readers of the annual report an insight into the results from normal trading. The extraordinary item itself will then be added to or deducted from the profit on ordinary activities after tax to show the actual profit for the year.

An expense has to satisfy three conditions before it can be treated as extraordinary. It must be:

● material,
● non-recurring, and
● resulting from an event which is totally outside normal business activities.

Each of these criteria must be applied to the particular circumstances of the company and the nature of the item itself. It has been suggested in the examples listed in the revised version of SSAP 6, for example, that redundancy costs are not extraordinary unless they have been incurred in respect of the discontinuance of an entire business segment. Gains or losses on the disposal of assets are not to be treated as extraordinary unless they have arisen from an extraordinary event such as an uninsured natural disaster.

Where an event is material and non-recurring but is not extraordinary because it resulted from a normal business activity, then it should be treated as an 'exceptional item'. If, for example, the company has suffered a large bad debt because of the unexpected collapse of a major customer, the cost of the debt written off should be accounted for as normal in the calculation of operating profit but disclosed in the note supporting the operating profit as 'exceptional bad debts'. This is because bad debts are regarded as being part of normal business activities, even if they are abnormally large. Other examples of exceptional items are the costs of large write-offs of stock or work-in-progress and redundancy costs in respect of the reduction of activity in a continuing business segment.

The distinction between extraordinary and exceptional items is a difficult one. To some extent, it should not be such a problem in examination questions because the examiner may feel obliged to exaggerate the nature of the problem in order to make it clear that he or she wishes to have it treated as extraordinary.

It is unusual to provide more than a brief statement of the nature of the extraordinary item in the notes to the profit and loss account. Most of the information given in the question is to enable candidates to decide whether the event was extraordinary or merely exceptional.

Progress Test 2

HIJ Ltd Trial Balance as at 31 December 19X2

	£000	£000
Debentures (10%)		120
Ordinary Share Capital (£1 shares)		300
Preference Share Capital (8%)		100
Share Premium		200
Profit and Loss Account		280
Patents and Trade Marks – Cost	270	
– Depreciation		70
Land and Buildings – Cost	300	
– Depreciation		40
Plant and Machinery – Cost	160	
– Depreciation		70
Vehicles – Cost	75	
– Depreciation		25
Computer – Cost	100	
– Depreciation		40
Debtors	195	
Creditors		98
Bank		40

	£000	£000
Cash	7	
Stock – Raw Materials	108	
– Work-in-Progress	34	
– Finished Goods	186	
Purchases – Raw Materials	760	
Manufacturing Wages	250	
Manufacturing Overheads	120	
Administration Expenses	160	
Selling and Distribution Costs	117	
Debenture Interest	12	
Interim Ordinary Dividend	10	
Suspense	300	
Sales		1,781
	3,164	3,164

1. Stocks at 31 December 19X2 were as follows:

	£000
Raw Materials	113
Work-in-Progress	38
Finished Goods	278
	429

2. Depreciation for the year is to be charged as follows:

Patents and Trade Marks	10% of cost
Land and Buildings	2% of cost
Plant and Machinery	20% of cost
Vehicles	20% reducing balance
Computer	30% of cost

Depreciation of land and buildings is to be apportioned two-thirds to production and one-third to administration.

The data-processing manager has estimated that 10% of the computer's running time is devoted to scheduling work for the production department and the remainder to clerical and administrative routines.

3. Manufacturing overheads include:

	£000
Plant Hire	14
Works Director's Salary	16

4. Administration expenses include:

	£000
Executive Directors' Salaries (two at £18,000 and one at £27,000)	63
Non-Executive Chairman's Fee	7
Auditor's Fees	19
Auditor's Expenses	4
Cost of Tax Advice Provided by Auditor	3

5. Selling expenses include the sales director's salary of £22,000.

6. The balance on the suspense account represents the cost of the assets lost and other expenses incurred when the assets of the company's Mordavian branch were seized following a military coup. This loss was uninsured.

7. The directors intend to pay the preference dividend and also a final ordinary dividend of £0.01 per share.

Solution to Progress Test 2

HIJ Ltd Profit and Loss Account for the Year Ended 31 December 19X2

	Notes	£000	£000
Turnover			1,781
Cost of Sales			(1,095)
Gross Profit			686
Distribution Costs		(127)	
Administrative Expenses		(189)	
			(316)
Operating Profit	[1]		370
Interest Payable			(12)
Profit on Ordinary Activities			358
Extraordinary Items	[3]		(300)
Profit for the Financial Year			58
Dividends	[4]		(21)
Profit Retained for the Year			37
Retained Profits brought forward			280
Retained Profits carried forward			317

HIJ Ltd Balance Sheet as at 31 December 19X2

	Notes	£000	£000
Fixed Assets			
Intangible Assets	[5]		173
Tangible Assets	[6]		382
			555
Current Assets			
Stocks	[7]	429	
Debtors		195	
Cash		7	
		631	
Creditors: Amounts falling due within one year	[8]	(149)	
Net Current Assets			482
Total Assets less Current Liabilities			1,037
Creditors: Amounts falling due after more than one year			
Debentures			(120)
			917
Capital and Reserves			
Called-up Share Capital	[9]		400
Share Premium Account			200
Profit and Loss Account			317
			917

Notes

1. Operating Profit
    Operating profit is arrived at after charging the following:

	£000
Plant Hire	14
Directors' Emoluments (note 2)	108
Auditor's Remuneration	23
Depreciation	105

2. Directors' Emoluments

	£000
Fees	7
Other Emoluments	101
	108

The emoluments of the chairman, excluding pension contributions, were £7,000 and those of the highest-paid director were £27,000.

The emoluments of the other directors, excluding pension contributions, fell within the following ranges:

£	Number
15,001 – 20,000	3
20,001 – 25,000	1

3. Extraordinary Item
   Assets costing £300,000 were expropriated by a foreign government.

4. Dividends

	£000
Proposed Preference Dividend	8
Interim Ordinary Dividend	10
Proposed Ordinary Dividend	3
	21

5. Intangible Fixed Assets
   Patents and Trade Marks

	£000
Cost	270
Aggregate Depreciation	97
	173

6. Tangible Fixed Assets

	Cost	Aggregate Depreciation	Net Book Value
	£000	£000	£000
Land and Buildings	300	46	254
Plant and Machinery	160	102	58
Vehicles	75	35	40
Computer	100	70	30
	635	253	382

7. Stock

	£000
Raw Materials	113
Work-in-Progress	38
Finished Goods	278
	429

8.   Creditors: Amounts falling due within one year

	£000
Bank Overdraft	40
Trade Creditors	98
Other creditors	11*
	149

* Proposed preference and ordinary dividends.

9.   Called-up Share Capital

	£000
Ordinary Shares of £1	300
8% Preference Shares	100
	400

Fixed Assets

The Companies Act also requires a detailed note regarding fixed assets. Rather than simply stating the closing balances on the cost and depreciation accounts, it is necessary to give a detailed summary of the movements which have occurred during the year.

The opening figures for the cost of fixed assets should be stated. The adjustments in respect of both additions and disposals should then be shown along with any other changes arising from revaluations. A similar set of details should be given in respect of depreciation, with the opening balances being adjusted by adding the annual depreciation charge and deducting the depreciation charged on disposals.

The value of land and buildings should be analysed to show the totals for freehold property, long leasehold (with 50 years or more unexpired) and short leasehold.

It is common practice to value land and buildings at their market value. This requires that the book value of the asset be increased to the revalued amount. The corresponding credit entry for this goes to a revaluation reserve, which becomes part of the shareholders' capital. Thus, if an asset which had cost £200,000 and had been depreciated by £40,000 was to be revalued at £500,000, the original cost would be replaced with a figure of £500,000. The depreciation charged to date would also be cancelled. This increase of £340,000 in the book value of the asset would be matched by an equivalent increase in the revaluation reserve.

Depreciation on revalued assets must be based on their balance sheet valuations.

The value of the assets which have been stated on another basis should be given, along with the year of revaluation, the name of the valuer and the method of valuation.

Illustration 4

A typical fixed asset note could appear as follows:

	Land and Buildings		Plant and Machinery	Total
	Freehold £000	Leasehold £000	£000	£000
Cost or Valuation				
1/1/X6	200	100	50	350
Additions	10	2	4	16
Disposals	(7)	(6)	(8)	(21)
31/12/X6	203	96	46	345
Depreciation				
1/1/X6	30	20	16	66
Charge for year	4	8	5	17
Disposals	(3)	(2)	(4)	(9)
31/12/X6	31	26	17	74
Net Book Value				
31/12/X6	172	70	29	271
1/1/X6	170	80	34	284

All assets are valued at cost except for freehold land and buildings, which were valued on an open market basis by Smith, Jones and Co., Chartered Surveyors.

Progress Test 3

Prepare, in a form suitable for publication, the profit and loss account and balance sheet of IJK plc.

IJK plc Trial Balance as at 31 December 19X8

	£000	£000
Ordinary Share Capital		5,000
Profit and Loss Account		2,900
Land and Buildings – Cost	4,500	
Plant and Machinery – Cost	2,800	
Fixtures and Fittings – Cost	1,500	
Depreciation – Land and Buildings		190
– Plant and Machinery		1,300
– Fixtures and Fittings		400
Investments in Loan Stock	2,100	
Interest Received from Loan Stock		220
Debenture Interest Paid	35	
14% Debenture Stock		500
Rental Income		160
Stocks as at 1 January 19X8	2,090	
Sales		20,467
Audit Fees	42	
Manufacturing Costs	10,400	
Distribution Costs	3,200	
Administration Costs	2,700	
Redundancy and Reorganisation	480	
Debtors	1,400	
Creditors		870
Bank	600	
Interim Dividend Paid	160	
	32,007	32,007

1. Stocks at 31 December 19X8 have been valued at £3,100,000.

2. Depreciation has still to be charged as follows:

Land and buildings	2% of cost
Plant and machinery	10% reducing balance
Fixtures and fittings	5% reducing balance

Depreciation of buildings is to be split 8:1:1 between manufacturing, administration and distribution.

Depreciation on plant and machinery is to be treated as a manufacturing cost, and depreciation of fixtures and fittings is to be treated as an administrative expense.

3.   The following transactions have been taken into account in arriving at the figures in the trial balance:

   ● Some plant was sold at its net book value of £200,000. This plant had originally cost £800,000.
   ● Plant and machinery costing £720,000 was acquired and £140,000 was spent on fixtures and fittings.

4.   The directors have proposed a final ordinary dividend of £320,000.

5.   Redundancy and reorganisation costs include £400,000 paid when the company closed a factory after it ceased production of that particular product line. A further £80,000 was paid to workers when the level of output was reduced at the main factory.

Solution to Progress Test 3

IJK plc Profit and Loss Account for the Year Ended 31 December 19X8

	Notes	£000	£000
Turnover			20,467
Cost of Sales			(9,692)
Gross Profit			10,775
Distribution Costs		(3,209)	
Administrative Expenses		(2,806)	
Other Operating Income		160	
			(5,855)
Operating Profit	[1]		4,920
Interest Receivable		220	
Interest Payable		(70)	
			150
Profit on Ordinary Activities			5,070
Extraordinary Items	[2]		(400)
Profit for the Financial Year			4,670
Dividends	[3]		(480)
Profit Retained for the Year			4,190
Retained Profits brought forward			2,900
Retained Profits carried forward			7,090

IJK plc Balance Sheet as at 31 December 19X8

	Notes	£000	£000
Fixed Assets			
Tangible Assets	[4]		6,615
Investments			2,100
			8,715
Current Assets			
Stocks		3,100	
Debtors		1,400	
Cash at Bank		600	
		5,100	
Creditors: Amounts falling due within one year	[5]	(1,225)	
Net Current Assets			3,875
Total Assets less Current Liabilities			12,590
Creditors: Amounts falling due after more than one year			
Debentures			(500)
			12,090
Capital and Reserves			
Called-up Share Capital			5,000
Profit and Loss Account			7,090
			12,090

Notes

1. Operating Profit
   Operating profit is stated after allowing for:

	£000
Auditor's Remuneration	42
Depreciation	295
Redundancy Costs	80
Rents Received	160

2. Extraordinary Item

	£000
Cost of Factory Closure	400

3. Dividends

	£000
Interim Dividend Paid	160
Proposed Final Dividend	320
	480

4.   Tangible Fixed Assets

	Land and Buildings £000	Plant and Machinery £000	Fixtures and Fittings £000	Total £000
Cost				
At 1/1/X8	4,500	2,880	1,360	8,740
Disposals	–	(800)	–	(800)
Additions	–	720	140	860
At 31/12/X8	4,500	2,800	1,500	8,800
Depreciation				
At 1/1/X8	190	1,900	400	2,490
Disposals	–	(600)	–	(600)
Charge	90	150	55	295
	280	1,450	455	2,185
Net Book Value				
At 31/12/X8	4,220	1,350	1,045	6,615
At 1/1/X8	4,310	980	960	6,250

5.   Creditors: Amounts falling due within one year

	£000
Trade Creditors	870
Accruals	35
Other Creditors	320
	1,225

Workings

Cost of Sales

	£000
Opening Stock	2,090
Manufacturing Costs	10,400
Redundancy Costs	80
Closing Stock	(3,100)
Depreciation – Buildings	72
– Plant	150
	9,692

Distribution Costs

	£000
Per Trial Balance	3,200
Depreciation – Buildings	9
	3,209

Administrative Expenses

	£000
Per Trial Balance	2,700
Auditor's Remuneration	42
Depreciation – Building	9
– Fixtures	55
	2,806

Fixed Assets

The opening balances are inferred by inserting the closing balances (which are obtained from the trial balance in the case of cost and the trial balance figures plus the charge for the year in the case of depreciation), the movements for the year, and then working backwards.

Disclosure of accounting policies

SSAP 2 requires that all of the company's major accounting policies be disclosed in a note to the financial statements. This enables the reader to ensure that any comparison which he wishes to make with another company's results will not be rendered misleading by differences between their accounting policies.

Any accounting policies which are described in the question should be listed in a final note. In the preceding question, for example, it would have been possible to provide two notes, one stating that the accounts have been prepared using the historical cost basis and the other describing the company's depreciation policy.

From a practical point of view, it is unlikely that many marks will be awarded to this part of the solution and it can take some time to write out all of the policies in some questions. For this reason, the accounting policies note should be left until last. If time does not permit this note to be fully completed then the policies which would have been discussed should be listed in order to demonstrate an awareness of the requirements.

Summary

Companies must publish accounting statements on an annual basis. These must comply with a variety of statutory and professional requirements.

The statements themselves must be laid out in accordance with detailed formats prescribed by the Companies Act. Abridged versions of these were provided in the body of the chapter. It is better to become accustomed to using these formats through practice than by attempting to memorise them.

The information in the statements must be supplemented by a large number of notes, the four most common of which were described. A description of the company's main accounting policies must also be provided.

4 Taxation in company accounts

Accounting for taxation is basically a simple matter. Limited companies must pay corporation tax on their profits. The amount of tax charged in any given year must be shown in the profit and loss account. Any amounts owing to the Collector of Taxes must appear as liabilities in the balance sheet. The problem is that the system by which corporation tax charges are calculated and subsequently collected is rather complicated.

This chapter will look at each of the following problems in turn:

- How is the amount of tax payable arrived at?
- When is this liability paid?
- What complications are created by the payment and receipt of dividends?
- What is 'deferred tax' and how is it accounted for?

It is important to grasp this topic because it is usually a major part of the numerical questions on the preparation of published accounting statements.

Objectives

This chapter will cover the following key objectives:

- The calculation of the tax charge in the profit and loss account and the liability in the balance sheet (see progress test 1)
- Accounting for the effects of dividends paid and received on the tax charge and the liabilities (see progress tests 2 and 3)
- Accounting for deferred taxation (see progress test 4)

The calculation of corporation tax

The corporation tax charge is based on the accounting figure for profits. It is not, however, a simple percentage of this amount. The legislation on corporation tax states that some sources of income which appear in the profit and loss account, such as certain types of government grant, are not taxable. Some expenses, such as depreciation or the cost of entertaining customers or suppliers, are not allowable for tax purposes. Equally, there are certain types of allowance which can be deducted from profit for tax purposes but which do not appear in the profit and loss account. The best example of this final type of adjustment are capital allowances, which are based on the cost of fixed assets and are, therefore, equivalent to a tax-deductible depreciation charge.

The first step, therefore, is to calculate the company's taxable profits. In practice, this is done by the company itself or by its professional advisers. This is because many of the rules contained in the legislation can be interpreted in a variety of different ways and some interpretations may be more favourable to the company than others. The Inland Revenue is, of course, entitled to disagree with the company's figures and the final calculation of the taxable profit figure is often a compromise.

Once the taxable profits have been agreed with the Inland Revenue, they must be multiplied by the appropriate percentage. While this may sound straightforward enough, the rate at which corporation tax is to be charged is announced in arrears during the Chancellor's annual budget. This means that the rate has to be estimated, usually by assuming that the previous year's rate will continue to be charged.

At the year end, the company's accountant must make assumptions about both the taxable profit and the corporation tax rate in order to arrive at the provision for tax which is to appear in the profit and loss account. This means, of course, that the amount provided will have to be adjusted once the final amount payable becomes known.

The calculation of taxable profit is rarely a problem in examination questions. Typically, the amount which is to be provided is simply stated in a note to the question.

The adjustment in respect of any under- or over-provision is made at the end of the following year. Any over-provision is deducted from the current year's estimated charge and any under-provision added.

Illustration 1

CDE plc estimated the tax charge on the profits for the year ended 31 December 19X6 at £500,000. During the following year, a charge of £490,000 was agreed with the Inland Revenue and paid to the Collector of Taxes.

The estimated charge on the profits for the year ended 31 December 19X7 is £680,000, based on an assumed corporation tax rate of 40%.

In the above case, the following note would appear in the annual report for the year ended 31 December 19X7:

Tax on Ordinary Activities

	£000
Corporation tax at 40%	680
Over-provision brought forward	(10)
	670

This means that a charge of £670,000 will appear in the profit and loss account, while an estimated liability of £680,000 will appear in the balance sheet. There are several reasons why the amount charged in the profit and loss account is different from the related liability in the balance sheet. In most questions, it is easier to calculate the two amounts independently.

Extraordinary Items

In the preceding chapter, it was pointed out that the profit figure should be calculated as if any extraordinary events had not occurred, in order to show how much profit has been generated from the company's normal trading activities. This figure should then be adjusted for the effects of the extraordinary activities.

The tax charge on ordinary activities should also be calculated as if the extraordinary event had not taken place. If this event has had any significance for tax purposes, the amounts shown in the note dealing with extraordinary items should show the gross value of the event and then adjust this for tax.

Care should be taken to include the effects of the extraordinary event when calculating the total liability for taxation.

Illustration 2

The estimated tax liability on FGH Ltd's ordinary activities for the year ended 31 December 19X5 is £800,000. This was based upon an estimated rate of 40%. An over-provision of £7,000 was made for the year ended 31 December 19X4.

During the year, the company closed down one of its major operating divisions. This cost £500,000, on which tax relief of £200,000 is expected.

The following notes would appear in the accounts of FGH Ltd:

Tax on Ordinary Activities

	£000
Corporation tax at 40%	800
Over-provision brought forward	(7)
	793

Extraordinary Item

	£000
Closure Costs	500
Taxation	(200)
	300

The balance sheet will show a liability of £600,000. This is arrived at by taking the amount which is actually expected to be paid in respect of the profits on ordinary activities (£800,000), and deducting the relief expected on the extraordinary costs (£200,000). The adjustment in respect of the over-provision has no effect on the final amount payable; it simply cancels a balance in the nominal ledger which is no longer necessary.

The payment of taxation

This section will look at the basic rules relating to the payment of tax, assuming that the company has neither paid nor received dividends. The payment of corporation tax is complicated by the effects of dividends. This complication will be dealt with in the section which follows.

Corporation tax must usually be paid within nine months of the company's year end. At one time, this period could vary between nine months and almost two years, although this particular anomaly has been phased out because of the provisions of the Finance Act 1987.

This means that the tax charge for the year will usually appear in the balance sheet as a current liability.

The trial balance will usually contain a balance in respect of corporation tax brought forward from the previous year. This is not a 'real' balance because it represents the under- or over-provision made in the previous year. (An under-provision will appear as a debit balance and an over-provision as a credit.)

The Companies Act format for the balance sheet makes provision for corporation tax under the sub-heading 'Other Creditors including Taxation and Social Security'. It is, however, necessary to ensure that the amount due in respect of taxation is disclosed separately from other creditors.

Progress Test 1

Prepare a profit and loss account and balance sheet, in a form suitable for publication, from the following information:

IJK plc Trial Balance as at 31 December 19X9

	£000	£000
Administrative Expenses	16	
Audit Fee	2	
Bank Overdraft		12
Cash	2	
Corporation Tax		3
Creditors		20
16% Debentures		50
Debenture Interest Paid	4	
Debtors	30	
Directors' Emoluments	18	
Distribution Costs	9	
Land and Buildings – Cost	250	
– Depreciation		30
Machinery – Cost	30	
– Depreciation		18
Vehicles – Cost	15	
– Depreciation		7
Profit and Loss Account		36
Provision for Bad Debts		1
Purchases	240	
Sales		353
Share Capital – Ordinary Shares of £1		190
Suspense	40	
Stock	47	
Wages and Salaries (Manufacturing)	17	
	720	720

1.   Stock was valued at £52,000 on 31 December 19X9, using the standard cost method.

2.   The following accruals have to be taken into account:

      Wages and Salaries   £1,000
      Administrative Expenses   3,000

3. Depreciation is to be charged as follows:

    Land and Buildings 2% of cost (manufacturing cost)
    Machinery   20% of cost (manufacturing cost)
    Vehicles   20% of cost (distribution expense)

4. It is IJK's policy to adjust the provision for bad debts to 10% of debtors at the year end.

5. The balance on the corporation tax account represents the over-provision made in respect of the profits for the year ended 31 December 19X8.

    The estimated corporation tax charge on the profits from ordinary activities of the current year is £18,000, based on an estimated rate of 40%.

6. The balance on the suspense account represents the cost of rectifying damage to the facade of a listed building by one of the company's delivery vehicles. The company's insurers have refused to meet this cost because the driver of the vehicle had not held an appropriate driving licence and the company had not taken sufficient care to check his credentials.

    It is expected that tax relief of £16,000 will be received as a result of this expense.

7. The company did not pay any dividends during the year, nor do the directors intend to propose any distribution.

8. There were no acquisitions or disposals of fixed assets during the year.

Solution to Progress Test 1

IJK plc Profit and Loss Account for the Year Ended 31 December 19X9

	Notes	£000	£000
Turnover			353
Cost of Sales			(264)
Gross Profit			89
Distribution Costs		(14)	
Administrative Expenses		(39)	
			(53)
Operating Profit	[1]		36
Interest Payable			(8)
Profit on Ordinary Activities			28
Tax on Profit on Ordinary Activities	[2]		(15)

	Notes	£000	£000
Profit on Ordinary Activities after Taxation			13
Extraordinary Item	[3]		(24)
Loss for the Financial Year			(11)
Retained Profits brought forward			36
Retained Profits carried forward			25

IJK plc Balance Sheet as at 31 December 19X9

	Notes	£000	£000
Fixed Assets			
Tangible Assets	[4]		226
Current Assets			
Stocks		52	
Debtors		27	
Cash		2	
		81	
Creditors: Amounts falling due within one year	[5]	(42)	
Net Current Assets			39
Total Assets less Current Liabilities			265
Creditors: Amounts falling due after more than one year	[6]		(50)
			215
Capital and Reserves			
Called-up Share Capital			190
Profit and Loss Account			25
			215

Notes

1.   Operating Profit
     Operating profit is stated after allowing for:

	£000
Auditor's Remuneration	2
Directors' Emoluments	18
Depreciation	14

(There is insufficient information in the question to permit any disclosure in respect of wages and salaries. Only the figures for manufacturing wages and the directors' emoluments have been provided.)

2.   Tax on Profit on Ordinary Activities

	£000
Corporation Tax at 40%	18
Over-provision brought forward	(3)
	15

3.   Extraordinary Item

	£000
Uninsured Accident	40
Tax Relief	(16)
	24

4.   Tangible Fixed Assets

	Land and Buildings	Machinery	Vehicles	Total
	£000	£000	£000	£000
Cost	250	30	15	295
Depreciation				
1 January 19X9	30	18	7	55
Charge for Year	5	6	3	14
31 December 19X9	35	24	10	69
Net Book Value				
31 December 19X9	215	6	5	226
1 January 19X9	220	12	8	240

5.   Creditors: Amounts due within one year

	£000
Bank Overdraft	12
Creditors	20
Accruals	8
Corporation Tax	2
	42

6.   Creditors: Amounts due after one year

	£000
Debentures	50

Accounting Policies

- The statements have been prepared under the historical cost convention.
- Stocks are valued at standard cost.
- Depreciation is calculated by the straight line method using the following rates:

Land and Buildings	2% per annum
Machinery and Vehicles	20% per annum

- A general provision amounting to 10% of gross debtors has been made.

Workings

Cost of Sales

	£000
Purchases	240
Opening Stock	47
Wages and Salaries (17 + 1)	18
Closing Stock	(52)
Depreciation – Land and Buildings	5
– Machinery	6
	264

Distribution Costs

	£000
Trial Balance	9
Depreciation – Vehicles	3
Increase in Provision for Bad Debts	2
	14

Administrative Expenses

	£000
Trial Balance	16
Audit Fee	2
Directors' Emoluments	18
Accrual	3
	39

Accruals

	£000
Wages and Salaries	1
Administration Expenses	3
Debenture Interest	4
	8

The current liability in respect of taxation comprises the estimated liability in respect of the current year's profit from ordinary activities of £18,000, less the tax relief on the extraordinary item of £16,000, leaving £2,000.

Dividends and advance corporation tax

The tax legislation requires that a company must pay part of its corporation tax liability in advance whenever it pays a dividend. The manner in which this rule is applied creates a number of accounting problems. These are dealt with by SSAP 8.

Payment of Advance Corporation Tax

Each year is divided into the following quarters:

1 January – 31 March
1 April – 30 June
1 July – 30 September
1 October – 31 December

If the end of the company's accounting period does not coincide with one of these quarters, then the appropriate quarter will be split into two.

At the end of each quarter, the company must account for any dividends paid or received. If a dividend has been paid during the year, then the company has to make a payment of 'Advance Corporation Tax' (ACT) within 14 days of the end of the quarter.

The amount of ACT is based on the basic rate of income tax. This is incorporated into the following formula:

$$\text{ACT Fraction} = \frac{\text{Basic Rate}}{100 - \text{Basic Rate}}$$

Thus, if the basic rate of income tax is 25%, the ACT fraction will be 25/75. If a company makes a dividend payment of £300,000 on, say, 19 August, it will have to pay ACT of £100,000 (£300,000 × 25/75) on 14 October.

Recovery of ACT

As the name suggests, ACT is, in theory, an advance payment of part of the total liability. In the normal course of events, this will be true. ACT on dividends paid during any given year can be offset against the final amount of tax payable for that year. Thus, ACT does not usually affect the total amount of tax payable, it merely alters the pattern of payment.

This may not, however, be the case. The company must pay ACT, even if it is unlikely that there will be any final liability against which to offset the advance. There are also upper limits on the amounts which can be reclaimed in any given year.

Illustration 2

In this case, none of the restrictions mentioned in the previous paragraph applies.

LMN plc made a final dividend payment of £210,000 in respect of the year ended 31 December 19X6. This was paid on 24 February 19X7. The company also paid an interim dividend of £360,000 on 17 September 19X7. At the end of the year, the directors have proposed a final dividend of £270,000.

The corporation tax on LMN's profits for the year has been estimated at £900,000.

The basic rate of income tax is 25%. The company must pay its corporation tax within nine months of the year end.

The corporation tax liability for the year ended 31 December 19X7 will be settled as follows:

		£000
14 April 19X7	ACT (£210,000 × 25/75)	70
14 October 19X7	ACT (£360,000 × 25/75)	120
30 September 19X8	Final payment (£900,000 − 70,000 − 120,000)	710
		900

Notice that it is the date on which the dividend is paid which matters. The date on which it is accrued is irrelevant, as is the fact that the payment may be from profits earned in a previous accounting period.

The final dividend for the year ended 31 December 19X7 was not actually paid during the year and has had no effect on the stream of payments for that year.

Notice that the ACT in respect of the dividend proposed at the end of 19X6 was not recovered until 30 September 19X8, a period of 21 months.

The balance remaining after part of the liability has been settled by the payment of ACT is called 'Mainstream Corporation Tax' (MCT).

Proposed Dividends

Whenever a dividend is proposed, a provision must be created for the related ACT liability. If the ACT is likely to be recovered, its expected recovery must also be shown as an asset. This entry may seem unnecessary because the asset and the liability would appear to cancel each other out. The point is, as was demonstrated in illustration 2 above, the payment of ACT in respect of the proposed dividend will be made within a few weeks of the year end while its recovery will take at least 21 months, and perhaps even longer.

Recoverable ACT can appear in one of two places in the balance sheet. It can either be offset against the liability of deferred taxation, a topic which will be covered later in this chapter, or it can be shown as a debtor in current assets. The first of these alternatives would appear to be preferred by SSAP 8, although there are other ways in which that particular requirement can be interpreted. If the latter treatment is adopted, the fact that the ACT will not be recovered within 12 months must be stated in the note relating to debtors.

Illustration 3

Taking the figures from illustration 2, the following balances would appear in the balance sheet in respect of tax:

	£000	£000
Current Assets		
. . .		
. . .		
Other Debtors		90
. . .		
. . .		
Creditors: Amounts due within one year		
. . .		
. . .		
Taxation		800
Proposed dividend		270
. . .		
. . .		

A note would warn that the £90,000 of other debtors was not recoverable within 12 months.

The liability in respect of taxation consists of the outstanding balance of £710,000 due for the current year, to which must be added the liability of £90,000 ACT which will become payable shortly after the year end, depending on when the final dividend is actually paid. There is no need to analyse the total of £800,000 to show how much is due for ACT and how much for MCT.

Dividends Received

The recipient of a dividend from a UK company is deemed to have received income in two ways. The amount of cash received is only part of the benefit.

Dividends are net of income tax at the basic rate and the shareholder is also deemed to have received a notional 'tax credit'. The tax credit is calculated using the same formula as that for the ACT fraction.

In order to ensure that the shareholder is charged the full amount of income tax which may be payable at the higher rates, he must declare the gross amount of his dividend on his income tax return. He will then be charged income tax at the appropriate rate, but can deduct the tax credit from his final assessment.

Illustration 4

Mr Q owns shares in RST plc. He received a dividend cheque for £300. Assuming that his income is not sufficient to take him into a higher tax band, he will be taxed on this amount as follows.

	£
Dividend Received	300
Tax Credit (£300 × 25/75)	100
	400
Tax at 25%	100
Less Tax Credit	(100)
Amount Payable	nil

This may seem cumbersome, but it ensures that taxpayers pay any higher rate tax in full. It also saves the Inland Revenue the task of collecting basic rate income tax from a large number of shareholders.

By definition, the total of the net dividend received and the tax credit is called 'Franked Investment Income' (FII).

Companies which own shares also receive tax credits. Unlike individuals, they cannot reclaim the tax credit in any way. Effectively, the company has paid income tax on its gross dividend income.

SSAP 8 requires that all investment income be shown gross and the amount of the irrecoverable tax credit be shown as part of the tax charge for the year. Thus, if a company had received a dividend of £300, it would have to show the gross total of £400 in its profit and loss account under the heading of 'Income from Investments'. The tax credit of £100 would then appear as 'Irrecoverable Tax Credits on Franked Investment Income' in the calculation of the tax charge on profits on ordinary activities. This may appear rather pedantic, given that the two adjustments will cancel each other out. The adjustments are necessary because the other sources of income in the profit and loss account are shown gross and it is desirable to show investment income in a consistent manner.

Any descriptions of dividends received must be read carefully to see whether the amounts shown are gross or net. Strictly, 'Dividends Received' usually refers to the net amount while 'FII' refers to the gross dividend.

Using Tax Credits

The company is entitled to offset the amount of tax credit received against the amount of ACT payable. In the long term, this ought to have no effect on the total amount of tax payable, but in the short term it will improve cash flows by delaying part of the advance payment.

It has already been pointed out that ACT is accounted for on a quarterly basis. If a surplus of FII arises in any given quarter, then it can be carried back to a previous quarter within the same accounting period and a repayment of ACT claimed from the Inland Revenue. The amount of any repayment is, however, restricted to the amount of ACT paid during the accounting period.

If a surplus of FII cannot be reclaimed because previous payments of ACT are insufficient then it may be carried forward and offset against dividend payments in future quarters or even future accounting periods.

Any dividends received during the year merit careful attention. Quite apart from the possible need to gross the amounts received in order to account for tax credits, there is also the possibility of an outstanding refund of some of the ACT paid during the year. Any such balance would have to be shown as a debtor.

Illustration 5

The following tables represent the receipts and payments of dividend for four unrelated companies. All amounts are shown net. Each company's financial year ends on 31 December 19X4. Each company is due to pay a total of £800,000 in corporation tax for the year and has proposed a final dividend of £210,000. The ACT fraction is 25/75.

RST Ltd

		Dividends Paid	Dividends Received
		£000	£000
Three months to	31/3/X4	240	180
	30/6/X4	–	–
	30/9/X4	360	–
	31/12/X4	–	–

RST Ltd will have paid ACT of £20,000 on the net payment of £60,000 for the first quarter and £120,000 on the payment made in the third. The balance sheet will show MCT due of £800,000 – 20,000 – 120,000 = £660,000. ACT payable and recoverable on the proposed dividend will amount to £70,000.

STU Ltd

		Dividends Paid	Dividends Received
		£000	£000
Three months to	31/3/X4	240	–
	30/6/X4	–	180
	30/9/X4	360	–
	31/12/X4	–	–

STU Ltd will have paid ACT of £80,000 on the first quarter's dividend, but will have reclaimed £60,000 of this after the second quarter. A further ACT payment of £120,000 after the third quarter means that MCT of £660,000 will be due at the year end and ACT payable and recoverable on the proposed dividend is still £70,000.

TUV Ltd

		Dividends Paid	Dividends Received
		£000	£000
Three months to	31/3/X4	240	–
	30/6/X4	–	–
	30/9/X4	360	–
	31/12/X4	–	180

TUV Ltd will have paid a total of £200,000 ACT on the dividends for the year. It will be able to recover £60,000 of this because of the FII received just before the year end. This amount will appear as a current asset at the year end. MCT will still equal £660,000 and the ACT on the proposed dividend will still be £70,000.

UVW Ltd

		Dividends Paid £000	Dividends Received £000
Three months to	31/3/X4	240	–
	30/6/X4	–	720
	30/9/X4	360	–
	31/12/X4	–	–

The £80,000 paid after the first quarter will have been recovered because of the FII received during the second. This will have left a surplus of £480,000 (£720,000 – 240,000) of FII to be carried forward. Part of the surplus will have been offset against the payment made in the third quarter, leaving no ACT to be paid. At the year end, MCT for the year will be £800,000 because no ACT has been paid during the year. The surplus FII received during the year amounts to £120,000. This can be carried forward to the next accounting period, reducing the ACT payable and recoverable on the proposed dividend to £30,000 ((£210,000 – 120,000) × 25/75 = £30,000).

In general, if a company has received FII, it should be assumed that any refund of ACT has already been received and accounted for unless the question contains a specific instruction to the contrary.

Progress Test 2

Using the information given below, prepare a profit and loss account and balance sheet for WXY plc in a form suitable for publication.

WXY plc Trial Balance as at 31 December 19X9

	£000	£000
Ordinary Share Capital		40
Sales		120
Manufacturing Costs	58	
Administrative Expenses	3	
Distribution Costs	4	
Tangible Fixed Assets – Cost	72	
– Depreciation		15

	£000	£000
Dividends Received (net)		6
Creditors		26
Stock at 31 December 19X9	9	
Debtors	39	
Investments (Long Term)	30	
Corporation Tax	1	
ACT	7	
Bank	11	
Dividends Paid	9	
Profit and Loss Account		36
	243	243

1. The balance on the corporation tax account represents the over-provision brought forward from the previous year.
2. The directors have proposed a final dividend of £15,000.
3. The company made a final dividend payment of £18,000 during the year. This was the amount proposed at the end of 19X8.
4. The tax charge for the year has been estimated at £17,000; this is based on an estimated rate of 40%.
5. Assume a basic rate of income tax of 25%.

Solution to Progress Test 2

WXY plc Profit and Loss Account for the Year Ended 31 December 19X9

	Notes	£000	£000
Turnover			120
Cost of Sales			(58)
Gross Profit			62
Distribution Costs		(4)	
Administrative Expenses		(3)	
			(7)
Operating Profit			55
Income from Investments			8
Profit on Ordinary Activities			63
Tax on Profit on Ordinary Activities	[1]		(20)
Profit on Ordinary Activities after Taxation		43	
Dividends	[2]		(24)
Profit Retained for the Year			19
Retained Profits brought forward			36
Retained Profits carried forward			55

WXY plc Balance Sheet as at 31 December 19X9

	Notes	£000	£000
Fixed Assets			
Tangible Assets			57
Investments			30
			87
Current Assets			
Stocks		9	
Debtors	[3]	44	
Cash at bank		11	
		64	
Creditors: Amounts falling due within one year	[4]	(56)	
Net Current Assets			8
Total Assets less Current Liabilities			95
Capital and Reserves			
Called-up Share Capital			40
Profit and Loss Account			55
			95

Notes

1. Tax on Profit on Ordinary Activities

	£000
Provision at 40%	17
Irrecoverable Tax Credits on FII	2
	19
Under-provision brought forward	1
	20

2. Dividends

	£000
Interim Dividend Paid	9
Final Dividend Proposed	15
	24

3. Debtors

	£000
Trade Debtors	39
Other Debtors	5
	44

Other debtors comprise recoverable ACT which will not be recovered within twelve months.

4.   Creditors: Amounts falling due
       within one year

	£000
Trade Creditors	26
Other Creditors	
– Proposed Dividend	15
– Tax	15
	56

Workings

1.   Income from Investments

	£000
Net Amount Received	6
Tax Credit at 25/75	2
Franked Investment Income	8

2.   Analysis of Balance on ACT Account

	£000
ACT Paid on 19X8 Final Dividend (£18,000 × 25/75)	6
ACT Paid on 19X9 Interim Dividend (£9,000 × 25/75)	3
ACT reclaimed after receipt of FII (£6,000 × 25/75)	(2)
	7

From this analysis, it can be seen that the total amount of ACT paid during the year is £7,000. This can be offset against the 19X9 MCT liability.

The analysis also shows that there is no outstanding balance or surplus in respect of the FII.

3.   Liability in Respect of Corporation Tax

	£000
Provision	17
ACT Paid during Year	(7)
MCT for year ended 31/12/X9	10
ACT Payable on Proposed Dividend (£15,000 × 25/75)	5 *
Total Liability	15

* This amount will also be recovered at a later date and is also shown as an asset.

Irrecoverable ACT

In any given year, the maximum amount of ACT which can be offset against a company's MCT liability is restricted. Effectively, the maximum amount which can be offset is equal to the company's taxable profit multiplied by the basic rate for income tax.

If the company is unable to reclaim all of its ACT in any given year, it may be able to carry the surplus back for up to two years and obtain a refund of any MCT payments made during this period. This type of claim is still subject to the upper limit which can be reclaimed in any given year and will be further restricted by the fact that part of this maximum may have already been used up. Any surplus which remains after this claim has been made may be carried forward indefinitely and offset against the MCT liability of future years, again subject to the same upper limit.

It would be quite possible for a company to pay dividends even although its taxable profits were very small, or even if it was making losses for tax purposes. This would mean that it would have a growing surplus of ACT which might never be reclaimed. In these circumstances, SSAP 8 requires that the company should take a realistic view of the value of this balance. If its recovery is not 'reasonably certain or foreseeable' then it should be written off as part of the current year's tax charge. The Standard suggests that it would not normally be prudent to carry a balance forward unless it is expected to be recovered within the next accounting period.

The right to recover ACT will continue, even if it has been written off for accounting purposes.

Progress Test 3

Prepare a profit and loss account and balance sheet for ZYX plc, in a form suitable for presentation to the shareholders.

ZYX plc Trial Balance as at 31 December 19X7

	£000	£000
Sales		511
Cost of Sales	160	
Administrative Salaries	18	
Directors' Remuneration	43	
Audit Fee	4	
Other Administrative Expenses	11	

	£000	£000
Selling and Distribution Expenses	5	
Share Capital (£1 shares, fully paid)		300
Hire of Sales Vehicles	12	
Loss on Closure of Office	42	
Interim Dividends	12	
Debtors	130	
Creditors		87
Investments	60	
Dividends Received		9
Bank	49	
Advertising	9	
ACT	60	
Freehold Factory Premises (at valuation)	321	
Revaluation Reserve		54
Plant and Equipment at Cost	114	
Vehicles at Cost (Directors' Company Cars)	97	
Depreciation for Year		
Factory	5	
Plant and Equipment	18	
Vehicles	21	
Accumulated Depreciation		
Factory		10
Plant and Equipment		38
Vehicles		44
Share Premium		50
12% Debentures		150
Debenture Interest	18	
Income from Sub-let of Factory Space		19
Stock at 31 December 19X7		
Raw Materials	30	
Work-in-Progress	56	
Finished Goods	32	
Corporation Tax		4
Profit and Loss Account		51
	1,327	1,327

1. The company's Belgian office was closed during the year. This was a branch office which coordinated all overseas sales, both within the EC and beyond. ZYX plc has now completely withdrawn from exporting.

    It is expected that tax relief of £13,000 will be received as a result of this expense.

2. Directors' remuneration comprises:

	Fees £000	Salary £000
Chairman and managing director	7	–
Finance director	2	18
Personnel director	2	14
	11	32

    Each director has a company car. The value of this benefit has been estimated at £2,000 for the chairman and £1,000 for each of the other directors.

3. During the year, plant and machinery which had cost £20,000 was sold for its net book value of £9,000.

    The chairman's car, which had cost £30,000 and which had been depreciated by £8,000, was sold and replaced by one costing £47,000.

    All of these transactions have been taken into account in arriving at the figures shown in the trial balance.

4. The balance on the corporation tax account represents the over-provision brought forward from the previous year. A provision of £39,000 is to be made for corporation tax on this year's profits from ordinary activities. This is based on an expected rate of 40%.

5. The large balance on the ACT account has arisen from the current year's transactions and also from a large dividend which was paid as part of reorganisation carried out in the previous year. This reorganisation has not generated the expected level of profits.

    The company is entitled to set up to £17,000 of ACT against the tax liability for the year ended 31 December 19X7. Any remaining surplus is unlikely to be reclaimed within the foreseeable future and should be written off.

6. The directors have proposed a final dividend of 11 pence per share.

7. The basic rate of income tax is 25%.

Solution to Progress Test 3

ZYX plc Profit and Loss Account for the Year Ended 31 December 19X7

	Notes	£000	£000
Turnover			511
Cost of Sales			(183)
Gross Profit			328
Distribution Costs		(26)	
Administrative Expenses		(97)	
Other Operating Income		19	
			(104)
Operating Profit	[1]		224
Income from Investments		12	
Interest Payable		(18)	
			(6)
Profit on Ordinary Activities			218
Tax on Profit on Ordinary Activities	[3]		(92)
Profit on Ordinary Activities after Taxation		126	
Extraordinary Items	[4]		(29)
Profit for the Financial Year			97
Dividends	[5]		(45)
Profit Retained for the Year			52
Retained Profits brought forward			51
Retained Profits carried forward			103

ZYX plc Balance Sheet as at 31 December 19X7

	Notes	£000	£000
Fixed Assets			
Tangible Assets	[6]		440
Investments			60
			500
Current Assets			
Stocks	[7]	118	
Debtors		130	
Cash at Bank		49	
		297	
Creditors: Amounts falling due within one year	[8]	(140)	
Net Current Assets			157
Total Assets less Current Liabilities			657
Creditors: Amounts falling due after more than one year			(150)
			507

	£000	£000
Capital and Reserves		
Called-up Share Capital		300
Share Premium Account		50
Revaluation Reserve		54
Profit and Loss Account		103
		507

Notes

1. Operating Profit
    Operating profit is arrived at after taking the following items into account:

	£000
Directors' Remuneration (note 2)	47
Auditor's Remuneration	4
Hire of Vehicles	12
Depreciation	44
Income from Rents	19

2. Directors' Remuneration

	£000
Fees	11
Other Emoluments	36
	47

    The chairman's total emoluments were £9,000 and those of the highest-paid director £21,000.
        In addition to these, one further director received total emoluments which were within the £15,001 to £20,000 range.

3. Tax on Profit on Ordinary Activities

	£000
Corporation Tax at 40%	39
Irrecoverable Tax Credits on FII	3
Recoverable ACT written off	54
	96
Over-provision brought forward	(4)
	92

4. Extraordinary Items

	£000
Closure Costs	42
Tax Relief thereon	(13)
	29

5. Dividend

	£000
Interim paid	12
Final proposed	33
	45

6. Tangible Fixed Assets

	Land and Buildings £000	Plant and Machinery £000	Vehicles £000	Total £000
Cost or Valuation				
At 1/1/X7	321	134	80	535
Additions	–	–	47	47
Disposals	–	(20)	(30)	(50)
At 31/12/X7	321	114	97	532
Depreciation at 1/1/X7	5	31	31	67
Disposals	–	(11)	(8)	(19)
Charge for year	5	18	21	44
At 31/12/X7	10	38	44	92
Net Book Value				
At 31/12/X7	311	76	53	440
At 1/1/X7	316	103	49	468

7. Stock

	£000
Raw Materials	30
Work-in-Progress	56
Finished Goods	32
	118

8.   Creditors: Amounts falling due within one year

	£000
Trade Creditors	87
Proposed Dividend	33
Taxation	20
	140

Workings

The figures for cost of sales, distribution costs and administrative expenses are all based on fairly obvious groupings of figures taken straight from the trial balance, and so the workings have not been reproduced.

The value of the directors' company cars have been included in the totals of their 'other emoluments'. These benefits are notional figures and have not been added to the total for administrative expenses.

ACT Written Off

	£000
Balance on ACT Recoverable Account	60
ACT Payable/Recoverable on Proposed Dividend	11
	71
Maximum ACT Recoverable within Foreseeable Future	17
Amount to be written off	54

The question stated that all of the surplus ACT had to be written off. If the forecast of future taxable profits and dividend payments had been different, it would have been perfectly acceptable for the company to have written off a smaller proportion of this balance.

Taxation Liability

	£000
Provision on Profits from Ordinary Activities	39
Tax Relief from Extraordinary Loss	(13)
	26
ACT offset	(17)
MCT due within one year	9
ACT on Proposed Dividend (£33,000 × 25/75)	11
Total Liability	20

Deferred tax

The adjustments in respect of deferred taxation are often misunderstood. This is unfortunate because the theory underlying it is extremely simple.

A liability comes into being whenever a business incurs an obligation to make a payment to a third party. If a company earns taxable profit, then it incurs a liability to the Collector of Taxes. In some cases, as has been seen in previous sections, this liability can be estimated with reasonable accuracy and will become payable within a relatively short time. Sometimes, there is a considerable delay between the creation of profit and the payment of tax. In some cases this delay can be for several years and may even be extended indefinitely.

These delayed payments are called 'deferred tax' and are dealt with by SSAP 15.

Timing Differences

Most of the differences between the accounting and taxable profits are permanent. Entertaining expenses, for example, are added back to the profit according to the profit and loss account and the company never receives any tax relief in respect of them.

Sometimes, the differences between the rules for the calculation of profit for accounting and tax purposes will lead to a transaction being recognised in the profit and loss account of one period and the tax computation of another. These differences are not permanent and will cancel themselves out with the passage of time.

Interest receivable, for example, is not taxed until it has actually been received. Assume that a company, which had no other sources of income, earned interest of £10,000 in year 1 but did not receive it until year 2. No interest was actually earned in year 2. This company would have no income for tax purposes in year 1, despite having earned the interest, but would have to declare year 1's interest in year 2. In these circumstances, it could not be considered correct to make provision for corporation tax in the normal manner. If the tax charge in year 1's profit and loss account is based directly on that year's tax computations then the liability in respect of the interest earned will be omitted from the financial statements. Year 2's tax charge will be inflated because of the effects of the interest received, even though the income was actually earned in an earlier period. Effectively, the profit after tax for year 1 will be overstated and that for year 2 will be understated. Furthermore, tax charges will not be deducted from their related profits. This disruption may prove misleading to the shareholders.

The solution to this problem is to recognise the liability as and when it is created. In year 1, the company has earned income which will lead to a tax charge of £4,000 (assuming a corporation tax rate of 40%) and so this charge will be recognised immediately, as will be the related liability to the Inland Revenue. This liability is not quite the same as a normal tax charge, which would be payable nine months after the year end, and so it is distinguished by describing it as 'deferred taxation'.

The tax note attached to the company's profit and loss account for year 1 will be as follows:

	£000
Corporation Tax	nil
Increase in Deferred Tax	4
	4

The Companies Act balance sheet format has a sub-heading for deferred tax which appears under the main heading of 'Provisions for Liabilities and Charges'. The liability of £4,000 at the end of year 1 would appear under this heading.

In year 2, the company would have to declare the income earned in year 1 and would be taxed accordingly. The accumulated totals of profit for tax and accounting purposes would, therefore, be brought back into line. Such differences are called 'timing differences'. When they are cancelled in this way they are said to 'reverse'. The tax note for year 2 would appear as follows:

	£000
Corporation Tax	4
Decrease in Deferred Tax	(4)
	nil

This would cancel out the balance on the deferred tax account.

The concept of deferred tax is analogous to the receipt of a loan from the tax authorities. For a variety of reasons, either to simplify the collection of tax or to provide an incentive for business, the tax laws may delay the charge to tax of certain profits, thereby granting a 'loan'. The deferred tax adjustment is simply required to ensure that the amount of this loan is recognised in the balance sheet. It also ensures that the amount of tax payable on the profits of any given year are matched against that year's profits, rather than deducting an artificial charge which has been deflated by recent 'advances' or inflated by 'repayments' of deferred tax.

'Permanent' Timing Differences

Timing differences can arise in a number of ways, not just as a result of the delay in the taxation of accrued interest. Capital allowances are effectively a form of depreciation which is allowable for tax purposes. These allowances are usually calculated in such a way that the cost of an asset is written off more quickly for tax than accounting purposes. This creates a timing difference which begins to reverse once the asset has been fully written off for tax purposes, but continues to depreciate in the profit and loss account. When a fixed asset is revalued, the amount of the revaluation may be recognised immediately in the financial statements, but no tax is charged on this gain until the asset is sold. This also results in a timing difference which only reverses on the sale of the asset.

The reversal of these timing differences may take some time to manifest themselves. Take the example of the revalued asset. Strictly speaking, the company will have incurred a liability to pay tax on the gain as soon as the increase in value occurred. It would be misleading, however, to recognise this liability in the balance sheet if the company had no intention of selling the asset in the foreseeable future.

SSAP 15 requires that a prudent view should be taken of the likely outcome of any timing differences which have arisen. No provision should be made if they are unlikely to reverse in the future. This is known as the 'partial provision' method.

The Mechanics of Accounting for Deferred Tax

It is impossible to calculate the amount which should be shown as the deferred tax balance without having access to a company's budgets covering its future profits, acquisition and disposal of fixed assets and so on. This means that examination questions must usually limit themselves to providing the opening balance on the deferred tax account in the trial balance and either stating the new closing balance or requiring that the existing balance be increased or decreased by a certain amount.

In the same manner as bad debt provisions, the movement for the year is shown in the profit and loss account as part of the tax charge, while the closing balance is shown in the balance sheet.

Recoverable ACT

If there is a recoverable ACT balance in respect of proposed dividends or a surplus of ACT being carried forward, SSAP 8 suggests that, wherever possible, this should be deducted from the deferred taxation balance instead of being shown as a current asset.

Corporation tax in the financial statements

It is worth recapitulating the various adjustments and balances which are required in respect of taxation before proceeding to the final progress test.

The charge in the profit and loss account will normally comprise the following items:

	£
Corporation Tax on Ordinary Activities	x
Irrecoverable Tax Credits on FII	x
Increase/(Decrease) in Deferred Tax	x
ACT written off	x
	x
Under/(over) – provision b/f	x
	x

Balances in respect of tax could appear under each of the main headings in the first half of the balance sheet, with the exception of fixed assets.

Current Assets
   Recoverable ACT (unless deducted from deferred tax)

Creditors: Amounts due within one year
   Current Year's Estimated MCT
   plus ACT Payable

Provisions for Liabilities and Charges
   Deferred Tax
   less Recoverable ACT.

Progress Test 4

Prepare a profit and loss account and balance sheet in a form suitable for publication from the following information:

WVU plc Trial Balance as at 31 December 19X5

	£000	£000
Sales		3,500
Purchases of Raw Materials	640	
Wages – Manufacturing	400	
– Administration	210	
– Distribution	170	

	£000	£000
Administration Costs	200	
Commissions Received		490
Selling and Advertising	240	
Manufacturing Overheads	370	
Opening Stocks – Raw Materials	185	
– Work-in-Progress	205	
– Finished Goods	320	
Interim Dividend	18	
Dividends Received		3
Taxation	7	
Property – Cost	600	
– Accumulated Depreciation		220
Plant and Machinery – Cost	1,400	
– Accumulated Depreciation		285
Disposal		12
Investments (Short Term)	14	
Bank		140
Overdraft Interest	17	
Bust Ltd	175	
Debtors	290	
Bad Debts	22	
Provision for Doubtful Debts		10
Creditors		160
Deferred Taxation		55
Share Capital		300
Share Premium		100
Profit and Loss Account		208
	5,483	5,483

1. Stocks at 31 December 19X5 were valued at their standard costs:

	£000
Raw Materials	260
Work-in-Progress	170
Finished Goods	410
	840

2. Plant and machinery is to be depreciated by 20% of cost.
    Property, which consists largely of the factory, is to be depreciated by 2% of cost.

3. The balance on the disposal account represents the proceeds from the sale of a machine which had cost £20,000 in 19X2. No further entries have been made in respect of this transaction.

    WVU plc charges a full year's depreciation in the year of acquisition and none in the year of disposal.

4. Just before the year end, the company had its property valued at £800,000 by Smith, Jones and Company, a firm of chartered surveyors. The directors have decided to bring this valuation into the balance sheet.

5. The following expenses have to be accrued:

	£000
Audit fee	11
Fees Payable to Five Non-executive Directors (£7,000 each)	35

6. The production director's salary of £19,000 is included in manufacturing overheads.

7. The sales director's salary of £17,000 is included in selling and advertising.

8. The managing director's salary of £22,000 and the chairman's salary of £15,000 are included in administration costs.

9. The provision for doubtful debts is to be increased by £2,000.

10. The balance on the Bust Ltd account is the cost of liquidating a loss-making subsidiary which had manufactured an obsolete product line which was unrelated to that of WVU plc.

    It is expected that tax relief of £70,000 will be obtained on this disposal.

11. The balance on the tax account consists of the net amount of ACT paid during the year, plus the balance remaining after the settlement of the previous year's assessment.

12. The balance on deferred tax is to be increased by £17,000.

13. Corporation tax of £460,000 is to be provided for the total taxable profit earned during the year.

14. The directors have proposed a final dividend of £36,000. Assume a basic rate of income tax of 25%.

Solution to Progress Test 4

WVU plc Profit and Loss Account for the Year Ended 31 December 19X5

	Notes	£000	£000
Turnover			3,500
Cost of Sales			(1,564)
Gross Profit			1,936
Distribution Costs		(434)	
Administrative Expenses		(456)	
Other Operating Income		490	
			(400)
Operating Profit	[1]		1,536
Income from Investments		4	
Interest Payable		(17)	
			(13)
Profit on Ordinary Activities			1,523
Tax on Profit on Ordinary Activities	[3]		(550)
Profit on Ordinary Activities after Taxation			973
Extraordinary Items	[4]		(105)
Profit for the Financial Year			868
Dividends	[5]		(54)
Profit Retained for the Year			814
Retained Profits brought forward			208
Retained Profits carried forward			1,022

WVU plc Balance Sheet as at 31 December 19X5

	Notes	£000	£000
Fixed Assets			
Tangible Assets	[6]		1,631
Current Assets			
Stocks	[7]	840	
Debtors		278	
Investments		14	
		1,132	
Creditors: Amounts falling due within one year	[8]	(849)	
Net Current Assets			283
Total Assets less Current Liabilities			1,914

	Notes	£000	£000
Provisions for Liabilities and Charges			
Deferred Tax	[9]		(60)
			1,854
Capital and Reserves			
Called-up Share Capital			300
Share Premium Account			100
Revaluation Reserve			432
Profit and Loss Account			1,022
			1,854

Notes

1. Operating Profit
    Operating profit is arrived at after charging for the following:

	£000
Wages	780
Depreciation	288
Auditor's Remuneration	11
Directors' Emoluments (note 2)	108

2. Directors' Emoluments

	£000
Fees	35
Other Emoluments	73
	108

    The Chairman's total emoluments were £15,000 and those of the highest-paid director were £22,000. The other directors received emoluments which fell within the following ranges:

£	Number
5,001 – 10,000	5
15,001 – 20,000	2

3. Tax on Profit on Ordinary Activities

	£000
Corporation Tax	530
Irrecoverable Tax Credits on FII	1
Transfer to Deferred Tax	17
	548
Under-provision brought forward	2
	550

4.　Extraordinary Item

	£000
Liquidation of Subsidiary	175
Tax Relief thereon	(70)
	105

5.　Dividends

	£000
Interim paid	18
Final proposed	36
	54

6.　Tangible Fixed Assets

	Property	Plant and Machinery	Total
	£000	£000	£000
Cost or valuation			
At 1 January 19X5	600	1,400	2,000
Disposal	–	(20)	(20)
Adjustment on Revaluation	200	–	200
At 31 December 19X5	800	1,380	2,180
Depreciation			
At 1 January 19X5	220	285	505
Disposal	–	(12)	(12)
Charge for Year	12	276	288
Adjustment on Revaluation	(232)	–	(232)
At 31 December 19X5	–	549	549
Net book value			
At 31 December 19X5	800	831	1,631
At 1 January 19X5	380	1,115	1,495

7.　Stock

	£000
Raw Materials	260
Work-in-Progress	170
Finished Goods	410
	840

8.   Creditors: Amounts due within one year

	£000
Bank Overdraft	140
Trade Creditors	160
Accrued Expenses	46
Proposed Dividend	36
Tax	467
	849

9.   Deferred Tax

	£000
Balance at 1 January 19X5	55
Transfer to Deferred Tax	17
	72
ACT recoverable	(12)
	60

Workings

Disposal

Disposal			
Cost	20	Bank	12
Gain on Disposal*	4	Depreciation	12
	24		24

*   Balancing figure.

The asset has been depreciated for three years (19X2, 19X3 and 19X4) at 20% of its cost each year. This means that £12,000 of depreciation must be cancelled on the disposal of this asset.

The disposal leaves assets costing £1,380,000. These are depreciated by 20% to give a charge for the year of £276,000. Both the charge for the year and the gain on disposal have been included in cost of goods sold.

Tax workings

The estimated tax charge is based on *total* profit and must be adjusted by adding back the tax relief on the extraordinary cost in order to arrive at the charge on ordinary activities of £530,000.

During the year, the company will have paid £6,000 ACT in respect of its interim dividend, of which £1,000 will have been reclaimed as a result of the tax credits on the FII. This means that a net payment of £5,000 has been made. This leaves a debit balance of £2,000 on the taxation account, which must be the amount of the under-provision from the previous year.

The tax liability at the year end consists of:

	£000
Corporation Tax Provision	460
ACT paid	(5)
MCT	455
ACT on Proposed Dividend	12
	467

Summary

Companies are required to pay corporation tax on their adjusted profits. This means that the charge must be shown in the profit and loss account and the related liabilities in the balance sheet.

The corporation tax charge is based on an estimate of the final agreed assessment. This must then be adjusted to reflect any irrecoverable tax credits, movements on deferred taxation, ACT written off and corrections to the previous year's estimate.

The balance sheet may contain several different balances in respect of taxation. The charge for the year will have to be paid, as will any ACT on proposed dividends. There may also be a liability in respect of deferred taxation.

There is very little direct link between the charge for corporation tax according to the profit and loss account and the amounts outstanding in the balance sheet.

The complexities of accounting for taxation arise because of the nature of the corporation tax system in the UK.

5 Consolidated financial statements

Three different accounting standards relate directly to the preparation of consolidated financial statements.

SSAP 14 deals with the most common situation, which is where the control of one company has been acquired by another. SSAP 14 requires the use of the so-called 'acquisition method'.

SSAP 23 deals with the case of two or more companies which have merged with each other. This is different from an acquisition in the sense that there is no dominant party involved and the shareholders of the two companies involved become joint owners of the new group. This continuation of ownership and control has accounting implications. SSAP 23 recommends the use of the 'merger method' in these circumstances.

SSAP 1 deals with the case of a company which can exert significant influence over another, but does not have outright control. Groups must use the 'equity method' in these circumstances.

This chapter will describe the application of the acquisition method as laid down in SSAP 14. This is the most complex of the three methods. The mechanics of the approach taken to it can be easily adapted to the application of the other two. The chapter will commence with a review of the basic concepts of consolidations. The consolidated balance sheet will be discussed with coverage given to the implications of pre-acquisition reserves, goodwill, minority shareholdings, inter-company balances and the revaluation of fixed assets. The consolidated profit and loss account will also be described.

Objectives

This chapter covers the following key issues:

- The preparation of the consolidated balance sheet (see progress test 1)

- Accounting for goodwill on consolidation (see progress test 2)
- Accounting for minority interests (see progress test 3)
- Inter-company balances and profits from inter-company trading (see progress test 4)
- Revaluation of assets on consolidation (see progress test 5)
- The preparation of the consolidated profit and loss account (see progress test 6)

Basic concepts

Large industrial organisations are often organised as groups of interrelated companies. There are a number of reasons why this may be so. Historically, the companies within the group could have been acquired as going concerns. The management of the controlling company could have felt that there were political or marketing considerations which would have made it unwise to transfer the assets of the controlled company to the acquirer and to liquidate the company itself.

The company which holds the controlling interest in the others is known as the 'holding company'. The companies which are controlled by the holding company are known as 'subsidiaries'. Collectively, a holding company and its subsidiaries are known as a 'group'.

Legally, the companies in the group retain their independence. In many cases, however, the business activities of the group members are closely related to one another, with group members supplying others with products or components or different group members manufacturing complementary product ranges. It is also common for group members to provide fellow members with finance. Even in the case of industrial conglomerates, where there is no direct link between the businesses of the members, all of the companies are under the control of the same senior management. It would be illogical for most purposes to view the group as being anything other than a single economic entity. The shareholders of the holding company will certainly be more interested in the performance of the group as a whole than they will be in that of the holding company taken on its own.

The holding company is required to publish a set of consolidated financial statements which reflect the economic reality of the group's existence. These requirements are enshrined by both the Companies Act 1985 and several of the SSAPs.

The holding company is obliged to publish a consolidated profit and loss account and balance sheet. These statements must comply with the format and disclosure requirements which apply to the individual companies.

The consolidated balance sheet

Basically, consolidation is a process of totalling the various items in the balance sheets of the individual group members. However, it must always be borne in mind that the purpose of the exercise is to present the statements as if the group was a single economic unit. Certain balances in the statements of the individual group members arise from relationships within the group and must be cancelled out before the figures can be meaningfully combined.

Illustration 1

H Ltd acquired 10,000 shares in S Ltd on 31 December 19X8. The balance sheets of the two companies at that date were as follows.

	H Ltd		S Ltd	
	£000	£000	£000	£000
Fixed Assets		8		6
Investment in S Ltd		10		–
Current Assets	12		10	
Current Liabilities	(10)		(6)	
		2		4
		20		10
Share Capital (£1 shares)		20		10

If this group is looked at from the outside, it can be seen that the directors of H Ltd control fixed assets with a book value of £14,000 (i.e. £8,000 + 6,000) and net current assets of £6,000 (i.e. £2,000 + 4,000). The calculation of the book value of the group's assets is, therefore, a simple matter of adding across the statements.

The capital section of the balance sheet is, however, less straightforward. S Ltd's balance sheet shows an obligation of £10,000 to its shareholder – H Ltd. This balance can be related directly to the £10,000 asset which appears in H Ltd's balance sheet. These balances arise out of an internal relationship within the group and is of no relevance to an outsider, not even to the shareholders of H Ltd. Thus, the two balances ought to be cancelled out against each other.

The consolidated balance sheet would appear as follows.

H Group Consolidated Balance Sheet as at 31 December 19X8

	£000	£000
Fixed Assets		14
Current Assets	22	
Current Liabilities	16	
		6
		20
Share Capital		20

The title states that this is a consolidated balance sheet. This is partly to differentiate it from the balance sheet of H Ltd itself, which will also have to be published. It is also important to warn the reader that the balance sheet relates to a group which may have economic reality but has no real legal substance. The group would not, for example, be responsible for the debts of a subsidiary company whose resources had become overstretched.

It is also worth noting that the balance sheet of the group must balance in the same manner as that of the individual companies. This means that it is often helpful to lay out the workings relating to the consolidation in the form of journal entries. In the example, the cancellation of the investment in S against S's share capital could be written out as:

Debit	Share Capital	£10,000
Credit	Investment in S	£10,000

This approach is used by accountants in practice. It also proves invaluable when dealing with more complicated examination questions.

Pre-acquisition profits

It must be remembered that the purchaser of ordinary shares is entitled to a share of the retained profits of the company. When cancelling out the intra-group balances, the amount paid for the shares must be offset against everything which was acquired, both share capital and reserves. This applies only to that part of the subsidiary's reserves which were purchased on the date when the shares were acquired. The reserves which arise after this date should be included in the reserves of the group.

Illustration 2

Assume, for example, that P Ltd acquired 10,000 shares in Q Ltd on 31/12/X3. The companies' balance sheets as at that date were as follows.

	P Ltd		Q Ltd	
	£000	£000	£000	£000
Fixed Assets		25		10
Shares in Q Ltd		13		–
Current Assets	8		7	
Current Liabilities	(6)		(4)	
		2		3
		40		13
Share Capital (£1 shares)		20		10
Profit and Loss Account		20		3
		40		13

Before combining the two balance sheets, it is necessary to cancel the £13,000 paid for the shares in Q Ltd against the obligation recorded by Q towards the holders of these shares. This requires the following journal entry:

Debit	Share Capital	£10,000
	Profit and Loss Account	3,000
	Credit Investment in Q Ltd	£13,000

The consolidated balance sheet will appear as follows.

P Group Consolidated Balance Sheet as at 31/12/X3

	£000	£000
Fixed Assets		35
Current Assets	15	
Current Liabilities	(10)	
		5
		40
Share Capital (£1 shares)		20
Profit and Loss Account		20
		40

The only reserves which are to be cancelled are those which were acquired when the shares were purchased in the subsidiary. For example, four years later, the balance sheets of the same two companies were as follows.

Balance Sheets as at 31 December 19X7

	P Ltd £000	P Ltd £000	Q Ltd £000	Q Ltd £000
Fixed Assets		34		19
Shares in Q Ltd		13		–
Current Assets	15		10	
Current Liabilities	(12)		(6)	
		3		4
		50		23
Share Capital (£1 shares)		20		10
Profit and Loss Account		30		13
		50		23

The value of the share capital and reserves acquired on 31/12/X3 are unchanged and so the journal entry to cancel out the intra-group balances will still be:

Debit	Share Capital	£10,000
	Profit and Loss Account	3,000
	Credit Investment in Q Ltd	£13,000

The consolidated balance sheet will appear as follows.

P Group Consolidated Balance Sheet as at 31/12/X7

	£000	£000
Fixed Assets		53
Current Assets	25	
Current Liabilities	(18)	
		7
		60
Share Capital (£1 shares)		20
Profit and Loss Account		40
		60

The consolidated reserves consist of the balance on the holding company's profit and loss account (£30,000), plus those earned by the subsidiary since it became a member of the group (£13,000 – 3,000 = £10,000). The group's reserves will always be restricted to those of the holding company plus the post-acquisition reserves of the subsidiaries, although some further adjustments may have to be made.

Progress Test 1

Prepare a consolidated balance sheet from the following information.

Balance Sheets as at 31 December 19X8

	H plc		S Ltd	
	£000	£000	£000	£000
Fixed Assets				
Tangible Assets				
Land and Buildings		250		60
Plant and Machinery		120		50
Fixtures and Fittings		70		10
		440		120
Investment in S Ltd		100		–
Current Assets				
Stocks	50		70	
Debtors	75		65	
Bank	20		65	
	145		200	
Current Liabilities	35		130	
Net Current Assets		110		70
		650		190
Long Term Loans		200		40
		450		150
Share Capital (£1 shares)		200		70
Share Premium		50		10
General Reserve		50		25
Profit and Loss Account		150		45
		450		150

H plc purchased 70,000 shares in S Ltd on 31 December 19X6. At that date, S Ltd's balance sheet stated that the balance on the general reserve was £5,000 and that on the profit and loss account was £15,000.

Solution to Progress Test 1

Workings

In 19X6, H acquired the share capital (including the share premium), the general reserve and the retained profits of S. The following journal entry is required to cancel out the inter-company balances which have arisen from this transaction:

Debit	Share Capital	£70,000
	Share Premium	10,000
	General Reserve	5,000
	Profit and Loss Account	15,000
Credit	Investment in S Ltd	£100,000

H Group Consolidated Balance Sheet as at 31 December 19X8

	£000	£000
Fixed Assets		
Tangible Assets		
Land and Buildings		310
Plant and Machinery		170
Fixtures and Fittings		80
		560
Current Assets		
Stocks	120	
Debtors	140	
Bank	85	
	345	
Current Liabilities	(165)	
Net Current Assets		180
		740
Long Term Loans		(240)
		500
Share Capital (£1 shares)		200
Share Premium		50
General Reserve		70
Profit and Loss Account		180
		500

The workings were shown before the consolidated balance sheet. This was deliberate. It is better to prepare the workings as one goes along in most practical accounting questions. Consolidations are, however, different. It is usually much better to prepare all of the workings before starting to draft the main statement. This is because most of the marks will be allocated to the small number of balances in the capital section of the balance sheet. Several adjustments may be required in order to arrive at these amounts. It is worth taking time to calculate these before drafting the statement itself.

Goodwill and capital reserves

So far, the illustrations have assumed that the amount paid for the subsidiary's shares and reserves is equal to their nominal value. There is no logical reason why this should be so. The amount paid for the shares would be a matter for negotiation between the buyer and the seller. The final price would be related to the profit which the company is expected to generate in the future, which has little to do with the book value of its assets.

Any amount paid in excess of the nominal value of the shares and reserves acquired by the holding company is known as 'goodwill'. In theory, this is the amount which the holding company is paying for such intangibles as the reputation of the subsidiary, its customer base and its loyal workforce. In the unlikely event that the holding company pays less for the subsidiary than the book value of its assets would suggest that it is worth, the discount is described as a 'capital reserve'.

Unless some other adjustment has been made, the balancing figure, whether it is goodwill or capital reserve, must be shown in the consolidated balance sheet. In terms of double entry bookkeeping, these balances must be shown, if only to make the statement balance. This treatment is acceptable if there is a capital reserve on acquisition, but not if there is goodwill.

The accounting treatment of goodwill is dealt with by SSAP 22. Essentially, this standard states that goodwill is not like other assets in that its value is difficult to measure objectively and may diminish over time. The standard states that goodwill on the acquisition of a subsidiary should be treated in either of two ways:

either   Goodwill ought to be written off immediately against reserves;
or   Goodwill ought to be amortised over its expected useful life.

The first of these treatments is preferred by the standard.

Illustration 3

Assume, for example, that T plc acquired all of the share capital in V Ltd on 31/12/X3.

Balance Sheets as at 31 December 19X3

	T plc £000	V Ltd £000
Fixed Assets	8	6
Investment in V Ltd	15	–
Net Current Assets	2	4
	25	10
Share Capital	22	8
Profit and Loss Account	3	2
	25	10

The adjustments which are required in respect of reserves on acquisition and the treatment of goodwill can become quite complex. The simplest means of avoiding errors is to use a 'T' account. This is often described as the 'cost of control' account.

The cost of control account and profit and loss accounts of T plc and V Ltd are as follows:

Cost of Control

Investment in V	15	Share Capital	8
		Profit and Loss	2
		Goodwill c/d	5
	15		15
Goodwill b/d	5		

There is a debit balance on the cost of control account. This means that T plc has paid a premium (goodwill) of £5,000 over the nominal value of the share capital and reserves acquired.

Profit and Loss

	T	V		T	V
Cost of Control	–	2	Bal b/d	3	2
Bal c/d	3	–			
	3	2		3	2
			Bal b/d (total)		3

The profit and loss account is separated into columns for each of the companies. Strictly, this is unnecessary when preparing the consolidated balance sheet. When preparing the consolidated profit and loss account, however, it is necessary to provide an analysis of the retained profit figure, stating how much belongs to the holding company and how much to the subsidiaries. It is useful practice to consider which member of the group should be charged or credited with any adjustments which affect reserves.

In the absence of a specific instruction in the question, one should always attempt to write goodwill off immediately against the group's reserves. This policy is preferred by SSAP 22. It would, however, be impossible to do so in this question because there are no post-acquisition reserves in the subsidiary's balance sheet and the holding company's reserves are inadequate. Thus the consolidated balance sheet would appear as follows.

T Group Consolidated Balance Sheet as at 31 December 19X3

	£000
Tangible Fixed Assets	14
Goodwill	5
Net Current Assets	6
	25
Share Capital	22
Profit and Loss Account	3
	25

If the cost of control account had had a credit balance, this would have meant that the subsidiary had been acquired at a discount. This balance would be shown as a 'Capital Reserve on Consolidation' amongst the other reserves in the consolidated balance sheet. Given that the value of a business as a going concern is likely to be greater than that of the assets listed in the balance sheet, it is unlikely that capital reserves will arise very often.

Illustration 4

The following example is rather more realistic. The holding company had sufficient reserves to enable it to write goodwill off immediately. The consolidation is being prepared some time after the date of acquisition, but note that the process of cancellation, including the calculation of goodwill, is based on the reserves as at the date when the shares in the subsidiary were acquired.

Big plc acquired 100% of the share capital of Small Ltd on 31/12/X5, when the balance on Small's profit and loss account was £3,000. Goodwill on the acquisition was written off immediately.

Balance Sheets as at 31 December 19X9

	Big plc £000	Small Ltd £000
Fixed Assets	16	9
Investment in Small Ltd	15	–
Net Current Assets	2	4
	33	13
Share Capital	14	7
Profit and Loss Account	19	6
	33	13

Workings (all figures in £000s)

Cost of Control

Investment in Small	15	Share Capital	7
		Profit and Loss	3
		Goodwill c/d	5
	15		15
Goodwill b/d	5	Profit and Loss	5

Profit and Loss

	Big	Small		Big	Small
Cost of Control	–	3	Bal b/d	19	6
Cost of Control	5	–			
Bal c/d	14	3			
	19	6		19	6
			Bal b/d		17

Big Group Consolidated Balance Sheet as at 31 December 19X9

	£000
Fixed Assets	25
Net Current Assets	6
	31

	£000
Share Capital	14
Profit and Loss Account	17
	31

The goodwill has been written off against the holding company's reserves on the grounds that the asset appears as part of the cost of the investment in the subsidiary in the holding company's balance sheet. There is no reason why the goodwill could not be written off against the reserves of another group member if the holding company's retained profit was inadequate for this purpose.

Progress Test 2

Prepare a consolidated balance sheet from the following information.

C Ltd acquired all of the share capital of D Ltd on 31/12/X1 when the balance on D Ltd's profit and loss account was £3,000.

Balance Sheets as at 31 December 19X4

	C Ltd		D Ltd	
	£000	£000	£000	£000
Fixed Assets				
Tangible		18		15
Investment in D		19		–
Current Assets	7		10	
Current Liabilities	(2)		(5)	
		5		5
		42		20
Share Capital		25		12
Profit and Loss		17		8
		42		20

Solution to Progress Test 2

Workings

Cost of Control

Investment in D	19	Share Capital	12
		Profit and Loss	3
		Goodwill c/d	4
	19		19
Goodwill b/d	4	Profit and Loss	4

Profit and Loss

	C	D		C	D
Cost of control	–	3	Bal b/d	17	8
Cost of control	4	–			
Bal c/d	13	5			
	17	8		17	8
			Bal b/d		18

C Group Consolidated Balance Sheet as at 31 December 19X4

	£000	£000
Fixed Assets		
Tangible		33
Current Assets	17	
Current Liabilities	(7)	
		10
		43
Share Capital		25
Profit and Loss		18
		43

Minority interests

It is unnecessary for the holding company to own all of the subsidiary's share capital in order for it to exercise control. In most circumstances, the holding company will have control if it owns 50% or more of the shares. (The definition of a subsidiary is rather moe complicated than this, but a detailed discussion of this topic would be outside the scope of this chapter.) Given that the directors of the holding company control all of the subsidiary's assets, it would not be appropriate to consolidate only that percentage which the holding company can claim to own. This leaves the problem of accounting for the portion of the subsidiary's finance which is provided by the other shareholders.

The value of the share capital and reserves provided by the subsidiary's minority shareholders is called the 'minority interest'. The minority interest must be shown separately in the balance sheet. The Companies Act formats require this to be shown in one of two places. It can be either deducted from the first part of the balance sheet (which deals with net assets) or shown in the capital section. In either case, the balance must appear at the end, just before the balance sheet total and must be disclosed separately. It would not really be appropriate to treat minority interest as a liability because it is not a loan. It would also be inappropriate to treat the minority interest as capital because the minority shareholders do not have the same interest in the operations of the group as the shareholders of the holding company.

Illustration 5

Assume, for example, that Q plc acquired 15,000 shares in R Ltd on 31 December 19X4. The balance on R's profit and loss account at that date was £8,000.

Balance Sheets as at 31 December 19X7

	Q plc		R Ltd	
	£000	£000	£000	£000
Fixed Assets		33		28
Investment in R Ltd		25		–
Current Assets	11		9	
Current Liabilities	(7)		(5)	
		4		4
		62		32
Share Capital (£1 shares)		40		20
Profit and Loss		22		12
		62		32

The cost of control account will be drafted in the usual way, taking care to compare the cost of the investment with the value of the share capital and reserves actually acquired. In this case, Q plc purchased 75% of the share capital of R Ltd.

Cost of Control

Investment in R	25	Share Capital	15 (75% of £20,000)
		Profit and Loss	6 (75% of £8,000)
		Goodwill c/d	4
	25		25
Goodwill b/d	4	Profit and Loss	4

The minority shareholders are entitled to 25% of the equity of R Ltd. At 31/12/X7 this amounts to £5,000 of the share capital and £3,000 of reserves. Note that there is no distinction between pre- and post-acquisition reserves when calculating the minority interest.

Minority Interest

		Share Capital	5 (25% of £20,000)
Bal c/d	8	Profit and Loss	3 (25% of £12,000)
	8		8
		Bal b/d	8

The calculation of the profit and loss account balance can become quite complicated because of the numbers of adjustments which have to be made to the figures in the individual companies' statements. One solution to this is to leave the profit and loss account until the end of the workings. It then becomes a simple matter to insert the balances as stated in the balance sheets and complete the double entry for those adjustments involving profit which have already been made in the other accounts.

Profit and Loss

	Q	R		Q	R
Cost of Control	–	6	Bal b/d	22	12
Cost of Control	4	–			
Minority Interest	–	3			
Bal c/d	18	3			
	22	12		22	12
			Bal b/d		21

Q Group Consolidated Balance Sheet as at 31 December 19X7

	£000	£000
Fixed Assets		61
Current Assets	20	
Current Liabilities	(12)	
		8
		69
Share Capital (£1 shares)		40
Profit and Loss		21
Shareholders' Funds		61
Minority Interest		8
		69

Progress Test 3

Prepare a consolidated balance sheet from the following information.

Exe plc acquired 16,000 shares in Wye Ltd on 30/6/X1 when the balance on Wye's general reserve was £5,000 and that on the profit and loss account was £25,000. Goodwill on acquisition was written off immediately against reserves.

Balance Sheets as at 30 June 19X4

	Exe plc		Wye Ltd	
	£000	£000	£000	£000
Fixed Assets				
Intangible		20		10
Tangible		80		43
Investment in Wye Ltd		50		–
		150		53
Current Assets	50		10	
Current Liabilities	(20)		(3)	
		30		7
		180		60
Debenture Loans		(50)		–
		130		60
Share Capital		80		20
Reserves				
General Reserve		20		10
Profit and Loss Account		30		30
		130		60

Solution to Progress Test 3

Workings

Cost of Control

Investment in Wye	50	Share Capital	16	(80% of £20,000)
		General Reserve	4	(80% of £5,000)
		Profit and Loss	20	(80% of £25,000)
		Goodwill c/d	10	
	50		50	
Goodwill b/d	10	Profit and Loss	10	

Minority Interest

		Share Capital	4	(20% of £20,000)
		General Reserve	2	(20% of £10,000)
Bal c/d	12	Profit and Loss	6	(20% of £30,000)
	12		12	
		Bal b/d	12	

General Reserve

Cost of Control	4	Bal b/d (Exe)	20
Minority Interest	2	Bal b/d (Wye)	10
Bal c/d	24		
	30		30
		Bal b/d	24

Profit and Loss

	Exe	Wye		Exe	Wye
Cost of Control	–	20	Bal b/d	30	30
Cost of Control	10	–			
Minority Interest	–	6			
Bal c/d	20	4			
	30	30		30	30
			Bal b/d		24

Exe Group Consolidated Balance Sheet as at 30 June 19X4

	£000	£000
Fixed Assets		
Intangible		30
Tangible		123
		153
Current Assets	60	
Current Liabilities	(23)	
		37
		190
Debenture Loans		(50)
		140
Share Capital		80
Reserves		
General Reserve		24
Profit and Loss Account		24
Shareholders' Funds		128
Minority Interest		12
		140

Inter-company balances

It has already been pointed out that all balances which exist between group members must be cancelled out before the financial statements can be consolidated. This would apply to any debtor or creditor balances which have arisen from trade between the companies in the group. This should be a straightforward matter of debiting creditors and crediting debtors with the amount outstanding. The problem is, however, that the two companies may disagree over the amount of the balance because of shipments of stock or cash payments in transit at the balance sheet date.

Illustration 6

The balance sheet extracts given below illustrate this problem.

	Hold Ltd		Sub Ltd	
	£000	£000	£000	£000
Current Assets				
Stock		50		30
Trade Debtors		60		45
Sub Ltd Current Account		10		–
Bank		8		7
		128		82
Current Liabilities				
Trade Creditors	(40)		(25)	
Hold Ltd Current Account	–		(3)	
		(40)		(28)
Net Current Assets		88		54

Subsequent investigation revealed that the difference between the current account balances was due to the following.

a.   Three days before the year end, Hold despatched stock to Sub. This stock was valued at £5,000. This stock did not arrive until after the year end.

b.   Four days before the year end, Sub sent a cheque for £2,000 to Hold. This cheque was still in the post on the balance sheet date.

The fact that these assets were in transit at the year end meant that the two current accounts disagreed by £7,000. More importantly, the figures for stock and bank were understated by £5,000 and £2,000 respectively. Neither company would have included the stock in its physical stocktaking at the end of the year. The cheque for £2,000 would have been removed from Sub's bank balance, but would not have been added to Hold's. The following journal entries would be required in order to correct these omissions:

Debit	Stock	£5,000
Credit	Sub Ltd Current Account	£5,000
Debit	Bank	£2,000
Credit	Sub Ltd Current Account	£2,000

Both of the adjustments have been made to the balance according to the holding company's ledger. It does not matter which set of records is changed, although in practice it may be more convenient for the holding company to make the alterations.

By this stage, the balances on each of the two current accounts will be £3,000. These can now be cancelled out by the following journal entry:

Debit	Hold Ltd Current Account	£3,000
Credit	Sub Ltd Current Account	£3,000

The working capital section of the consolidated balance sheet would appear as follows:

	£000	
Current Assets		
Stock	85	(i.e. 50 + 30 + 5)
Trade Debtors	105	
Bank	17	(i.e. 8 + 7 + 2)
	207	
Current Liabilities		
Trade Creditors	65	
Net Current Assets	142	

Unrealised Profits on Inter-company Trading

When group members trade with each other, there is no reason why sales should not be made at the normal selling price. In the normal course of events, goods sold by one group member to another will have been resold to a third party by the balance sheet date. In the following series of transactions, for example, a consignment of stock which had cost £50 was sold by the holding company to a subsidiary for £70. This consignment was then resold by the subsidiary for £80.

	Holding Company's Books	Subsidiary Company's Books
Selling price	£70	£80
Cost	50	70
Profit	20	10

When the accounts of the two companies are consolidated, they will show a total profit of £30 on the above series of transactions. This makes sense because the stock cost the group £50 and it has been sold for £80.

Unfortunately, there could be problems if the stock had remained unsold at the end of the year.

	Holding Company's Books	Subsidiary Company's Books
Selling price	£70	
Cost	50	£70
Profit	20	

In this case, the consolidated statements would show a profit of £20 on the inter-company sale and would value the stock at £70. This is illogical. If the group is to be seen as a single economic entity, it cannot generate profits by selling goods to itself. Nor should it value stock at more than its original cost.

The solution is to calculate the value of unrealised profits included in stock at the year end and cancel this out as follows:

Debit	Profit and Loss Account	£20	
Credit	Stock		£20

Progress Test 4

Prepare a consolidated balance sheet from the following information.

H plc acquired 80% of the share capital of I Ltd on 1 January 19X4.

The balance sheets of H plc and I Ltd were as follows as at 31 December 19X6.

	H plc		I Ltd	
	£000	£000	£000	£000
Fixed Assets				
Tangible				
Land and Buildings		54		77
Plant and Machinery		70		26
		124		103
Investment in I Ltd		150		–
		274		103
Current Assets				
Stock	40		35	
Debtors	80		45	
I Ltd Current a/c	22		–	
Bank	5		6	
	147		86	
Current Liabilities				
Creditors	(65)		(38)	
Taxation	(15)		(9)	
H plc Current a/c	–		(7)	
	(80)		(54)	
Net Current Assets		67		32
		341		135
Share Capital		200		75
Profit and Loss Account		141		60
		341		135

Notes

1. There was a balance of £40,000 on I Ltd's profit and loss account at 1 January 19X4.

2. Goodwill on acquisition was written off immediately against reserves.

3. I Ltd sent H plc a cheque for £3,000 during December 19X6. This did not arrive until January 19X7.

4. H plc despatched stock with an invoiced value of £12,000 in December 19X6. This was not received until after the year end. H plc made a profit of £3,000 on this sale.

5. I Ltd's closing stock at 31 December 19X6 includes goods which had been purchased from H plc for £8,000. The profit element included in this amount was £1,000.

Solution to Progress Test 4

Workings

1.

Cost of Control			
Investment	150	Share Capital	60
		(80% of £75,000)	
		Profit and Loss	32
		(80% of £40,000)	
		Goodwill c/d	58
	150		150
Goodwill b/d	58	Profit and Loss	58

2.

Minority Interest			
		Share Capital	15
		(20% of £75,000)	
Bal c/d	27	Profit and Loss	12
		(20% of £60,000)	
	27		27
		Bal b/d	27

3. Cash in Transit
Debit	Bank	£3,000
Credit	I Ltd Current a/c	£3,000

4. Stock in Transit
Debit	Stock	£12,000
Credit	I Ltd Current a/c	£12,000

5. Inter-company Balances
    The foregoing adjustments mean that each company's records will show the inter-company balance as £7,000. Now that the balances agree, they can be cancelled:

Debit	H plc Current a/c	£7,000
Credit	I Ltd Current a/c	£7,000

6. Unrealised Profit
    There is unrealised profit of £3,000 included in I's closing stock and of £1,000 included in stock in transit.

Debit	Profit and Loss Account	£4,000
Credit	Stock	£4,000

7.

Profit and Loss

	H	I		H	I
Cost of Control	–	32	Bal b/d	141	60
Cost of Control	58	–			
Minority Interest	–	12			
Stock	–	4			
Bal c/d	83	12			
	141	60		141	60
			Bal b/d		95

Any adjustments in respect of unrealised profit on inter-company sales is usually deducted from the subsidiary's profits regardless of which company made the sale. This is in order to ensure that the analysis of group profits is correct. When taking the holding company and treating it as a company in its own right, it is legitimate to argue that it has sold the stock at a profit.

H Group Consolidated Balance Sheet as at 31 December 19X6

	£000	£000
Fixed Assets		
Tangible		
Land and Buildings		131
Plant and Machinery		96
		227
Current Assets		
Stock	83	
Debtors	125	
Bank	14	
	222	
Current Liabilities		
Creditors	(103)	
Taxation	(24)	
	(127)	
Net Current Assets		95
		322
Share Capital		200
Profit and Loss Account		95
Shareholders' Funds		295
Minority Interest		27
		322

Revaluation of assets on consolidation

SSAP 22 defines goodwill as the difference between the value of the business as a whole and the fair value of the assets of its separable net assets. This means that, under acquisition accounting, the possibility of the fair value of the subsidiary's assets being significantly different from their book value must be considered. Any reserve on revaluation must be taken into account in the calculation of goodwill. The fair values of the assets must also be included in the consolidated balance sheet.

It is important to consider the impact of this revaluation on the depreciation charge when calculating group profit. Depreciation must be based on the revalued amount.

Illustration 7

K plc acquired 80% of the share capital of L Ltd on 31 December 19X5. The book value of L Ltd's plant and machinery was £100,000 at that date. The fair value of this plant and machinery was £150,000 at that date. The remaining useful life of the plant and machinery was estimated at 10 years. L Ltd's profit and loss account showed a balance of £200,000 as at 31 December 19X5.

The balance sheets of the companies as at 31 December 19X6 were as follows. Neither company had purchased or sold any fixed assets during the year.

	K plc £000	L Ltd £000
Fixed Assets		
Land and Buildings	300	160
Plant and Machinery	240	90
	540	250
Investment in L Ltd	270	–
	810	250
Net Current Assets	50	40
	860	290
Share Capital	450	60
Profit and Loss Account	410	230
	860	290

Cost of Control

Investment	270	Share Capital	48 (80% of £60,000)
		Profit and Loss	160 (80% of £200,000)
		Plant and Machinery	40 (80% of £50,000)
		Goodwill c/d	22
	270		270
Goodwill b/d	22	Profit and Loss	22

In this example, the fair value of the subsidiary's assets exceeded their book value by £50,000 on acquisition. The holding company is entitled to 80% of this surplus on revaluation.

The revaluation of the assets will require an additional annual depreciation charge of £5,000 (i.e. £50,000/10). This additional charge will be recorded by means of the following journal entry:

Debit   Profit and Loss   £4,000
               Minority Interest   1,000
    Credit   Plant and Machinery   £5,000

Note that the group is entitled to only 80% of the revaluation surplus and so it is only expected to bear 80% of the additional depreciation charge. The remaining 20% is charged to the minority shareholders. This adjustment should not be seen as unfair to the minority. Their rights will be fully reflected in the subsidiary's balance sheet and they will not suffer any loss whatsoever as a result of this debit entry to their account.

Remember that the amount of the adjustment in respect of additional depreciation required on the revalued amount will be the cumulative depreciation to date since the acquisition.

Plant and Machinery

Bal b/d – K	240	Profit and Loss	4
Bal b/d – L	90	Minority Interest	1
Cost of Control	40		
Minority Interest	10	Bal c/d	375
	380		380
Bal b/d	375		

Minority Interest

Plant and		Share Capital	12 (20% of £60,000)
Machinery	1	Profit and Loss	46 (20% of £230,000)
Bal c/d	67	Plant and Machinery	10
	68		68
		Bal b/d	67

Profit and Loss

	K	L		K	L
Cost of Control	–	160	Bal b/d	410	230
Cost of Control	22	–			
Plant and Machinery	–	4			
Minority Interest	–	46			
Bal c/d	388	20			
	410	230		410	230
			Bal b/d	408	

K Group Consolidated Balance Sheet as at 31 December 19X6

	£000
Fixed Assets	
Land and Buildings	460
Plant and Machinery	375
	835
Net Current Assets	90
	925
Share Capital	450
Profit and Loss Account	408
Shareholders' Funds	858
Minority Interest	67
	925

Progress Test 5

The balance sheets of G plc and M Ltd at 31 December 19X7 were:

	G plc		M Ltd	
	£000	£000	£000	£000
Fixed Assets				
Tangible				
Plant and Machinery		140		90
Equipment		26		6
Investment in M Ltd		110		–
		276		96
Current Assets				
Stock	36		24	
Debtors	128		42	
Bank	20		11	
	184		77	
Current Liabilities				
Creditors	(73)		(23)	
		111		54
		387		150
Share Capital		300		100
Profit and Loss		87		50
		387		150

1. G acquired 60% of the share capital of M on 31 December 19X5 when the balance on M's profit and loss account was £30,000.
2. A piece of plant owned by M, which had a book value of £50,000 on 31 December 19X5, was valued at £70,000 at that date. The estimated useful life of this asset was four years from the date of revaluation.
3. M's closing stock includes goods obtained from G for £10,000. G had sold these for cost plus 25%.
4. G's debtors figure includes a balance of £4,000 payable by M. M's creditors figure includes a liability due to G of £1,000. The difference is due to a cheque for £3,000 which was in transit at the balance sheet date.

Solution to Progress Test 5

Cost of Control

Investment	110	Share Capital	60	(60% of £100,000)
		Profit and Loss	18	(60% of £30,000)
		Plant & Machinery	12	(60% of £20,000)
		Goodwill c/d	20	
	110		110	
Goodwill b/d	20	Profit and Loss	20	

Additional depreciation will be required on the revalued asset. This will amount to £5,000 per annum (£20,000/4). The revaluation took place two years ago and so an additional £10,000 (£5,000 × 2) of depreciation will be required.

Debit	Profit and Loss	£6,000	
	Minority Interest	4,000	
Credit	Plant and Machinery		£10,000

Plant and Machinery

Bal b/d – G	140	Profit and Loss	6
Bal b/d – M	90	Minority Interest	4
Cost of Control	12		
Minority Interest	8	Bal c/d	240
	250		250
Bal b/d	240		

The unrealised profit on M's closing stock amounts to £2,000 (i.e. £10,000 × 25/125). This will be cancelled as follows:

Debit	Profit and Loss	£2,000
Credit	Stock	£2,000

The cash in transit at the end of the year will be recorded as follows:

Debit	Bank	£3,000
Credit	Debtors (M Ltd)	£3,000

The inter-company balances can now be cancelled:

Debit	Creditors (G plc)	£1,000
Credit	Debtors (M Ltd)	£1,000

Minority Interest

Plant and Machinery	4	Share Capital	40 (40% of £100,000)
		Profit and Loss	20 (40% of £50,000)
Bal c/d	64	Plant and Machinery	8 (40% of £20,000)
	68		68
		Bal b/d	64

Profit and Loss

	G	M		G	M
Cost of Control	–	18	Bal b/d	87	50
Cost of Control	20	–			
Plant and Machinery	–	6			
Stock	2	–			
Minority Interest	–	20			
Bal c/d	65	6			
	87	50		87	50
			Bal b/d		71

G Group Consolidated Balance Sheet as at 31 December 19X7

	£000	£000
Fixed Assets		
Tangible		
Plant and Machinery		240
Equipment		32
		272
Current Assets		
Stock	58	
Debtors	166	
Bank	34	
	258	
Current Liabilities		
Creditors	(95)	
		163
		435
Share Capital		300
Profit and Loss		71
Shareholders' Funds		371
Minority Interest		64
		435

Consolidated profit statement

The same basic approach is taken to the consolidation of the profit statement as to the preparation of the group balance sheet. The group is still viewed as a single economic entity and the basic mechanics involve totalling the balances of the various group members. Obviously, it is still necessary to cancel any transactions which have occurred between group members, particularly inter-company trading and inter-company dividends.

Where there is a minority interest in the profits of the group, this is dealt with as follows, assuming that the figures are listed in the order laid down by the Companies Act format.

1. Starting at turnover and working down to profit on ordinary activities after tax, calculate the total amounts for the group. These figures should, of course, be adjusted for any inter-company transaction.

2. Calculate the minority interest in the group profit on ordinary activities and show this as a deduction from group profit. The minority share of

the subsidiary's profit should be adjusted to reflect any alterations to the subsidiary's profit figure such as additional depreciation charges on revalued assets.

3.   All subsequent figures should be expressed in terms of the percentage to which the holding company is entitled. If, for example, a subsidiary which was 75% owned had suffered an extraordinary loss, the group profit statement would include only 75% of this amount in the total for extraordinary losses.

Illustration 8

X plc paid £400,000 for 90% of Y Ltd's share capital on 31 December 19X2. Y Ltd's paid-up share capital amounted to £200,000 at that date and the balance on its profit and loss account was £150,000. Y Ltd had no other reserves.

It is X plc's policy to write off goodwill on acquisition immediately against reserves.

The profit and loss accounts of the two companies for the year ended 31 December 19X6 are set out below.

	X plc £000	Y Ltd £000
Turnover	898	740
Cost of Sales	(420)	(400)
Gross Profit	478	340
Investment Income	8	–
	486	340
Administration Expenses	(220)	(85)
Distribution Costs	(90)	(46)
Profit on Ordinary Activities	176	209
Taxation	(70)	(59)
Profit on Ordinary Activities after Taxation	106	150
Extraordinary Losses (net of tax)	10	30
Profit for the Financial Year	96	120
Dividends	(45)	(60)
Retained Profit for the Year	51	60
Retained Profit brought forward	480	300
Retained Profits carried forward	531	360

1. During the year, X made sales to Y of £100,000. These goods had originally cost X £80,000. At the end of the year, 20% of this consignment of stock was still unsold.

2. X's investment income consists of its share of Y's interim dividend.

Workings

It is necessary to calculate the amount of goodwill written off on acquisition.

Cost of Control

Investment	400	Share Capital	180 (90% of £200,000)
		Profit and Loss	135 (90% of £150,000)
		Goodwill c/d	85
	400		400
Goodwill b/d	85	Profit and Loss	85

The trading between the group members must also be cancelled out:

Debit   Sales   £100,000
  Credit   Cost of Sales   £100,000

The unrealised profit on the stock supplied to Y by X amounts to £4,000 (i.e. £20,000 × 20%). This is cancelled as follows:

Debit   Cost of Sales   £4,000
  Credit   Stock   £4,000

The inter-company dividend creates the final problem. The holding company is entitled to total investment income of £54,000 (90% of £60,000). Only £8,000 has been recorded. X's share of the proposed final dividend will have to be accrued as follows:

Debit   Debtors (Y Ltd)   £46,000
  Credit   Investment Income   £46,000

The dividend paid by Y cannot, of course, be treated as income generated by the group and so it will have to be cancelled:

Debit Investment Income   £54,000
  Minority Interest   6,000
  Credit Dividends   £60,000

The minority shareholders will be credited with their full share of the subsidiary's profit for the year. The payment of part of this in the form of a dividend will effectively reduce the amount of finance which they have provided to the group and so they will have to be debited.

The retained profits according to the consolidated profit and loss account has to be analysed to show how much is held within the holding company and how much is in the subsidiaries. Note that it is calculated in two stages. The balances brought forward are adjusted to reflect any adjustments made on acquisition or in respect of additional depreciation charged during the period prior to the commencement of the current year. Entries are then required to show the current year's profit and the adjustments which have to be made to it.

Profit and Loss

	X	Y		X	Y
Cost of Control	–	135	Retained		
Cost of Control	85	–	Profit b/f	480	300
Minority Interest	–	30*			
Bal c/d	395	135			
	480	300		480	300
Stock	–	4	Bal b/d	395	135
Minority Interest			Retained Profit		
in Profit for Year	–	12	for Year	51	60
			Debtors (Y)	46	–
Dividends	–	54	Investment Income	–	60
Bal c/d	492	185			
	492	255		492	255
			Bal b/d	492	185

*   10% of £300,000

The adjustment in respect of minority interest in the profits of the year is based upon the profit after tax and extraordinary items. This does not correspond immediately to the figure stated in the consolidated profit statement, which is shown gross of extraordinary items and then adjusted by bringing a reduced percentage of the extraordinary items into the consolidated profit statement.

The debit entry for the cancellation of the investment income in respect of inter-company dividends has been put into the subsidiary company's column. This is because it is common practice to treat the dividend as having been earned by the holding company for purposes of the analysis of retained profit. There is no theoretical reason why this entry should not be made in the holding company's profit and loss account.

The holding company must publish its own balance sheet in addition to that of the group. It need not, however, publish its own profit and loss account in addition to the consolidated statement. It is sufficient to publish a note which says that the company is exercising its right not to publish its own statement and states the amount of the profit on ordinary activities after tax which is dealt with in the holding company's profit statement. In the case of X plc, profit on ordinary activities after tax was £106,000, to which has to be added the accrued dividend from Y to give a total of £152,000.

X Group Consolidated Profit and Loss Account for the Year Ended 31 December 19X6

	£000	
Turnover	1,538	(i.e. 898 + 740 − 100)
Cost of Sales	(724)	(i.e. 420 + 400 − 100 + 4)
Gross Profit	814	
Administration Expenses	(305)	
Distribution Costs	(136)	
Profit on Ordinary Activities	373	
Taxation	(129)	
Profit on Ordinary Activities after Taxation	244	
Minority Interests	(15)	(i.e. $150 \times 10\%$)
	229	
Extraordinary Losses (net of tax)	(37)	(i.e. 10 + 90% of 30)
Profit for the Financial Year	192	
Dividends	(45)	
Retained Profit for the Year	147	
Retained Profit brought forward	530	(i.e. 395 + 135)
Retained Profits carried forward	677	
Retained in Holding Company	492	
Retained in Subsidiaries	185	
	677	

As permitted under Section 228(7) of the Companies Act 1985, the profit and loss account of the parent company is not presented as part of these accounts. The consolidated profit on ordinary activities after tax includes £152,000 which is dealt with in the profit and loss account of X plc.

Progress Test 6

You are required to prepare a consolidated profit statement for the year ended 31 December 19X4 for A plc and its subsidiary Z Ltd:

	A plc £000	Z Ltd £000
Turnover	800	700
Cost of Sales	(550)	(370)
Gross Profit	250	330
Administrative Expenses	(100)	(80)
Distribution Costs	(40)	(30)
	110	220
Investment Income	40	–
	150	220
Taxation	(70)	(105)
Profit on Ordinary Activities after Tax	80	115
Extraordinary Loss	(30)	(15)
	50	100
Dividend	(24)	(50)
Retained Profit for Year	26	50
Retained Profit brought forward	300	280
Retained Profit carried forward	326	330

1. A paid £500,000 on 31 December 19X1 for 80% of Z's share capital of £200,000. The balance on Z's profit and loss account was £250,000 at that time.

2. On the date of acquisition, a manufacturing asset which had a book value of £100,000 was found to have a fair value of £150,000. This asset had an estimated useful life of 10 years.

3. A made sales to Z which were worth a total of £200,000 during the year. Not all of the goods had been resold by the year end. The profit element included in Z's closing stock was £20,000.

4. The figure for investment income in A's profit statement comprises the holding company's share of the subsidiary's total dividend for the year.

Solution to Progress Test 6

Cost of Control

Investment	500	Share Capital	160	(80% of £200,000)
		Profit and Loss	200	(80% of £250,000)
		Plant and Machinery	40	(80% of £50,000)
		Goodwill c/d	100	
	500		500	
Goodwill b/d	100	Profit and Loss	100	

Depreciation on Revalued Assets

Additional depreciation will have been charged and deducted for the two years ended 31 December 19X3. This will amount to £10,000 and will be recorded as follows when calculating the retained profit brought forward:

Debit	Profit and Loss	£10,000
Credit	Fixed Assets	£10,000

The additional charge for the year ended 31 December 19X4 will be recorded as follows.

Debit	Profit and Loss	£5,000
Credit	Fixed Assets	£5,000

Inter-company Sales

Debit	Turnover	£200,000
Credit	Cost of Sales	£200,000

Unrealised Profit

Debit	Cost of Sales	£20,000
Credit	Stock	£20,000

Subsidiary Dividends

These will be cancelled as follows.

Debit	Investment Income	£40,000
	Minority Interest	10,000
Credit	Dividends	£50,000

Analysis of Retained Profits

The minority interest in the profits brought forward amounts to £54,000 (i.e. 20% of £280,000 = £56,000, less the minority share of the additional depreciation charge of £2,000).

The minority interest in the profits for the year amounts to £19,000 (i.e. 20% of £100,000 = £20,000, less the minority share of the additional depreciation charge of £1,000).

Profit and Loss

	A	Z		A	Z
Cost of Control	–	200	Retained Profit		
Cost of Control	100	–	brought forward	300	280
Fixed Assets	–	10			
Minority Interest	–	54			
Bal c/d	200	16			
	300	280		300	280
Stock	–	20	Bal b/d	200	16
Fixed Assets	–	5	Retained Profit		
Investment Income	–	40	for Year	20	50
Minority Interest	–	19	Dividends	–	50
Bal c/d	220	32			
	220	116		220	116
			Bal b/d	220	32

A Group Consolidated Profit and Loss Account for the Year Ended 31 December 19X4

	£000	
Turnover	1,300	(800 + 700 – 200)
Cost of Sales	(745)	(550 + 370 – 200 + 20 + 5)
Gross Profit	555	
Administrative Expenses	(180)	
Distribution Costs	(70)	
	305	
Taxation	(175)	
Profit on Ordinary Activities after Tax	130	
Minority Interest	(22)	(20% of (115 – 5))
	108	

	£000	
Extraordinary Loss	(42)	(80% of 15 + 30)
	66	
Dividend	(30)	
Retained Profit for Year	36	
Retained Profit brought forward	216	
Retained Profit carried forward	252	

As permitted under Section 228(7) of the Companies Act 1985, the profit and loss account of the parent company is not presented as part of these accounts. The consolidated profit on ordinary activities after tax includes £80,000 which is dealt with in the profit and loss account of A plc.

Summary

The purpose of a set of consolidated financial statements is to portray the group as if it were a single economic entity. This requires that the figures which appear in the individual statements be combined. Common sense dictates that a number of adjustments will have to be made to cancel out any transactions or balances between members of the group.

This chapter has described the approach which should be taken to the preparation of the balance sheet and profit and statement of a group of companies using the acquisition method. The basic approach taken would be equally suitable for the preparation of statements under merger and equity accounting, which are, in fact, simpler to apply.

The secret to completing these statements in the shortest possible time and with the lowest possibility of error is to make ample use of the simple concept of double entry bookkeeping. All adjustments should be thought out in terms of journal entries with 'T' accounts used to organise the workings for the more complex figures. A set of neat, methodical workings, prepared before starting to draft the statement itself, will save time and will simplify the question enormously.

It is usually wise to leave all consideration of the profit figure until the end of the workings. This means that the correct figure can be obtained by opening an account and entering the converse entries to those adjustments which have already been made.

6 Practical bookkeeping

Double entry bookkeeping was discussed in Chapter 1. That chapter did not go beyond the basic mechanics of the technique because students preparing to take an examination in financial accounting do not require a more detailed knowledge. Anyone who is planning to study auditing does, however, require a slightly deeper insight into how an accounting system actually works.

This chapter will describe the manner in which businesses maintain their accounting records. The initial recording of routine transactions and the way in which they are summarised for subsequent recording will be considered. The division of the various tasks involved in record keeping will be described, with some emphasis placed on the prevention of fraud and error. Finally, an outline will be given of some of the implications of the computerisation of accounting systems.

Objectives

The following key issues are covered in this chapter:

- The recording of transactions in the initial records and in the nominal ledger (see progress test 1)
- The drafting of journal entries (see progress test 2)

Initial recording of transactions

Routine transactions such as sales, purchases, and the receipt and payment of cash must be recorded on an almost constant basis. It would be both difficult and undesirable to record each transaction separately in the nominal ledger. In a manual system, there would be too many entries for one person to record and it would be impractical to have several people working on the same ledger. Furthermore, some of the accounts, such as bank or sales, would contain so many entries that they would be difficult to balance off. Even if the system was computerised, keeping all of the accounting data on one file would create processing problems.

It is also undesirable to keep all of the debtors' and creditors' accounts within the nominal ledger. Most businesses will have many customers and suppliers. An accurate record must be kept of the amount owed by or to each one. It is usually necessary for at least one employee, sometimes several, to be engaged on this task on a full-time basis for each of debtors and creditors.

All but the smallest of businesses will summarise the basic transactions in a series of day books. Only the totals from these need to appear in the relevant accounts in the nominal ledger. There will also be separate ledgers for debtors and creditors, with only summarised accounts appearing in the nominal ledger itself.

The Sales Cycle

A typical credit sale will be recorded as follows.

- Details of the customer's requirements are taken down on a prenumbered order form.
- Once the customer's credit rating has been checked, the goods will be manufactured or taken from stock. Before they are sent to the customer, a prenumbered despatch note will be raised. Several carbon copies of this will usually be created. One copy will be sent to the customer with the goods. A second copy will be signed by the customer and returned to the company as a receipt. A third copy will be used to create an invoice. Further copies may be used to update stock records or for analysis by the marketing department.
- The accounts department will record the details from the third copy of the despatch note on to a prenumbered invoice. Again, carbon copies will be created. One copy will go to the customer and at least one copy will be retained by the company for accounting purposes.
- The copy invoice will be recorded in the sales day book. This is just a list of sales invoices, usually in numerical order. There will be columns for the net value of the sale, the related Value Added Tax (VAT) and the gross value.
- On a regular basis, perhaps monthly, the total sales figure for the month will be recorded by debiting the debtors' control (or total) account and crediting sales. Thus, the sales account may have only 12 entries in any year, one for each month. The individual sales will also be recorded in the customers' accounts in the sales (or debtors') ledger.

This system is designed in such a way that it would be difficult to omit anything, either accidentally or deliberately. The prenumbering of the various documents means that they cannot be lost or suppressed without this being detected.

The company has to keep a record of each customer's balance for credit control purposes. The sales ledger is just a collection of debtors' accounts. These can be laid out in exactly the same way as the accounts in the nominal ledger itself, although some additional details, such as invoice numbers, may be recorded against each transaction. The individual entries in the sales day book will be debited to the relevant account in the sales ledger. The sales ledger is not part of the nominal ledger and so there is no need to maintain double entry in respect of any transactions recorded in it.

The debtors' control account is part of the nominal ledger. It is used to keep a record of the total amount owed by debtors and so it is only necessary to enter the total from the sales day book each month. This account is usually referred to as the 'sales ledger control account'.

This arrangement reduces the number of accounts in the nominal ledger. It also enables a certain amount of cross-checking to be carried out. At the end of each month, the total of the balances on the sales ledger can be compared with the balance on the sales ledger control. The two figures have been derived from the same basic information and should agree. The sales ledger and nominal ledger will normally be maintained by different members of staff. If one has made an error, or even fraudulently falsified his records, this will be detected because the two totals will not be equal.

Illustration 1

ABC plc commenced trading on 1 January 19X3. During its first month of trading it made four sales: £100 to Brown on the 7th, £200 to Blue on the 12th, £150 to Green on the 18th, and £80 to Brown on the 26th. None of these goods were paid for during the month. All of ABC's sales are exempt from VAT. These transactions would be recorded as follows.

1. Sales Day Book

		£
7/1/X3	Brown	100
12/1/X3	Blue	200
18/1/X3	Green	150
26/1/X3	Brown	80
		530

2.   Nominal Ledger

Sales Ledger Control

31/1/X3	Sales Day Book	530	31/1/X3	Bal c/d	530
		530			530
1/2/X3	Bal b/d	530			

Sales

			31/1/X3	Sales Day Book	530

3.   Sales Ledger

Blue

12/1/X3	Sales Day Book	200	31/1/X3	Bal c/d	200
		200			200
1/2/X3	Bal b/d	200			

Brown

7/1/X3	Sales Day Book	100			
26/1/X3	Sales Day Book	80	31/1/X3	Bal c/d	180
		180			180
1/2/X3	Bal b/d	180			

Green

18/1/X3	Sales Day Book	150	31/1/X3	Bal c/d	150
		150			150
1/2/X3	Bal b/d	150			

The total of the three balances on the sales ledger is £530, which agrees with the balance on the sales ledger control account.

If the sales day book had been totalled up incorrectly, this would have had no effect on the recording of the individual transactions in the sales ledger, although the entry in the control account would have been incorrect. Thus, the two figures would have disagreed and an investigation would have discovered the error. Similarly, if the clerk in charge of the sales ledger had deliberately omitted the sale to, say, Green from his account in the sales ledger, perhaps so that he could steal Green's payment and conceal the theft, the balance on the control account would have been unaffected while the total of the sales ledger balances would have been reduced, again prompting an investigation.

Purchases Cycle

A typical purchase would be recorded as follows.

- The purchasing department would be warned of the need to replenish stocks of a certain item.
- The purchasing department would find the most appropriate supplier and would send a written order, using an official, prenumbered form. A carbon copy would be kept in the buying department and another would be passed to accounts.
- The supplier would deliver the goods. The stores department would record the delivery on a prenumbered goods-received note. Carbon copies of this would be sent to purchasing and to accounts.
- The supplier would invoice the company for the goods. The staff in the accounts department would ensure that the goods had been both ordered and received by checking the details on the invoice against their copy of the order form and the goods-received note.
- The invoice would be recorded in the purchase day book. This is simply a list of all purchases on credit, with columns for the net value of the goods, the related VAT, and the gross value of the invoice.
- On a regular basis, often monthly, the total of the month's purchases according to the purchase day book would be debited to purchases and credited to the creditors' ledger control account. The individual entries in the purchase day book would be entered into their relevant accounts in the purchase ledger.

The function of the creditors' (or 'purchase ledger') control account is very similar to that of the sales ledger control account. It is used to calculate the total amount owed to the company's creditors. This account is supported by the purchase ledger, which gives the amount owed to each supplier. The total of the balances on the purchase ledger should always agree with the balance on the control account.

This system is both efficient and capable of reducing the likely incidence of fraud. Each aspect of the transaction is controlled by staff from different departments. There would be little point in the purchasing staff trying to order goods for their own use because the deliveries are made to stores. The stores section records all goods on prenumbered documents; this ensures that the inventory records are subsequently updated. The stores staff would find it difficult to abuse their access to the stock because it must be recorded on delivery, otherwise the accounts staff will not record the invoice and the goods will not be paid for. The accounts department staff maintain the records, but do not have access to the stocks. This separation of the authorisation of transactions, custody of the related assets and responsibility for recording them is known as 'segregation of duties'.

Receipts and Payments

Most companies will be continually receiving payments from customers and making payments for materials, wages and other expenses. These transactions will be recorded in the cash book and only summaries will appear in the nominal ledger. Each side of the cash book is usually divided into columns so that the various types of receipts and payments can be analysed.

A typical layout for a cash book is as follows.

Illustration 2

Receipts Side

Date	Description	Amount	Debtors	Cash Sales	Sundries
		£	£	£	£
1/2	Balance b/f	2,000			
7/2	Green	150	150		
9/2	Cash sale	40		40	
12/2	Blue	200	200		
16/2	Brown	180	180		
22/2	Rent from sub-let	90			90
27/2	Cash sale	60		60	
		2,720	530	100	90

Payments Side

Date	Cheque number	Description	Amount	Creditors	Wages	Sundries
			£	£	£	£
3/2	12345	Smith	50	50		
6/2	12346	Jones	120	120		
14/2	12347	Wages	1,100		1,100	
22/2	12348	Rent	250			250
26/2	12349	Harris	70	70		
28/2	Bal c/f		1,130			
			2,720	240	1,100	250

The company had £2,000 in the bank at the start of the month. During the month it received a total of £720 from various sources and made a number of payments worth £1,590. These transactions would be recorded in the nominal ledger as follows.

Debit	Bank		£720	
	Credit	Sales Ledger Control		£530
		Cash Sales		100
		Income from Sub-let		90
Debit	Purchase Ledger Control		£240	
		Wages	1,100	
		Rent	250	
	Credit	Bank		£1,590

This means that the account for bank in the nominal ledger will be adjusted to the correct balance of £1,130 on 28 February.

The various receipts from customers and payments to suppliers will also be recorded in the relevant accounts in the sales and purchase ledgers.

Usually, the maintenance of the cash book is the responsibility of the cashier. The cashier would also be responsible for the preparation of cheques and for dealing with any balances of petty cash.

Most receipts will come in the form of cheques from customers. All mail should be opened in the presence of at least two people, neither of whom should be responsible for either the cash book or the sales ledger. All cheques should be registered in a note book and details of the amounts received passed to the cashier and the clerk in charge of the sales ledger. This is another application of the concept of segregation of duties. The cashier and the sales ledger clerk could be in a position to steal cheques from customers and alter their records to conceal the theft. This is not, however, possible because the amounts received according to the cheque register can be compared with the amounts lodged according to the bank statements and any discrepancies investigated.

The system for payments is just as simple. Most routine payments will be for purchases and wages. The cashier will be notified of these, and also of any non-routine payments, by the relevant departments. Claims for payment should be supported by documentary evidence such as invoices or a payroll. The cashier will then write out cheques as required and will pass these on for signature.

Most businesses require that their cheques be signed by two senior managers or directors. These signatories should compare the details on the cheque with the supporting documentation. Once the cheque has been signed, the documents should be stamped or initialled to show that they have been paid and to prevent them from being submitted twice. The cheques will then be posted to their payees or, in the case of wages, cashed.

Progress Test 1

Record the following transactions in the sales and purchase day books and the cash book. Use these records to update the sales and purchase ledgers, their respective control accounts and the bank account in the nominal ledger.

1 March   The following balances are to be brought forward at the start of the month:

	Debtors	Creditors
	£	£
Aye Ltd	200	
Bee plc		170
See plc	120	
Dee plc	400	
Eff Ltd		240
Gee Ltd	320	
Jay plc		290
Kay plc		160
Emm Ltd	410	
	1,450	860

There was a balance of £3,400 in the current account at 1 March.

3 March	Bought £200 of goods on credit from Eff Ltd. Sold £160 to See plc.
4 March	Paid wages of £600.
7 March	Made sales of £500 to See plc and £250 to Dee plc. Paid £100 to Eff Ltd and £100 to Jay plc.
11 March	Paid wages of £590.
15 March	Aye Ltd settled the balance on its account.
16 March	Cash sales £120.
18 March	Paid wages of £620.
19 March	Purchased £340 from Kay plc and £70 from Jay plc.
22 March	Made sales of £150 to Dee plc and £90 to Gee Ltd.
24 March	Received £120 from See plc, £400 from Dee plc and £350 from Emm Ltd.
25 March	Paid £170 to Bee plc, £120 to Eff Ltd and £220 to Kay plc.
26 March	Paid wages of £610.
29 March	Cash sales £360.
	Ignore VAT.

Solution to Progress Test 1

Sales Day Book (SDB)

		£
3 March	See plc	160
7 March	See plc	500
7 March	Dee plc	250
22 March	Dee plc	150
22 March	Gee Ltd	90
		1,150

Purchase Day Book (PDB)

		£
3 March	Eff Ltd	200
19 March	Kay plc	340
19 March	Jay plc	70
		610

Cash Book (CB)

Receipts

Date	Details	Amount	Debtors	Cash Sales
		£	£	£
1/3	Bal b/f	3,400		
15/3	Aye Ltd	200	200	
16/3	Sales	120		120
24/3	See plc	120	120	
24/3	Dee plc	400	400	
24/3	Emm Ltd	350	350	
29/3	Sales	360		360
		4,950	1,070	480
1/4	Bal b/f	1,820		

Payments

Date	Details	Amount	Creditors	Wages
		£	£	£
4/3	Wages	600		600
7/3	Eff Ltd	100	100	
7/3	Jay plc	100	100	
11/3	Wages	590		590
18/3	Wages	620		620
25/3	Bee plc	170	170	
25/3	Eff Ltd	120	120	
25/3	Kay plc	220	220	
26/3	Wages	610		610
31/3	Bal c/f	1,820		
		4,950	710	2,420

Sales Ledger

Aye Ltd

1/3	Bal b/d	200	15/3	CB	200

See plc

1/3	Bal b/d	120	24/3	CB	120
3/3	SDB	160			
7/3	SDB	500	31/3	Bal c/d	660
		780			780
1/4	Bal b/d	660			

Dee plc

1/3	Bal b/d	400	24/3	CB	400
7/3	SDB	250			
22/3	SDB	150	31/3	Bal c/d	400
		800			800
1/4	Bal b/d	400			

Gee Ltd

1/3	Bal b/d	320			
22/3	SDB	90	31/3	Bal c/d	410
		410			410
1/4	Bal b/d	410			

Emm Ltd

1/3	Bal b/d	410	24/3	CB	350
			31/3	Bal c/d	60
		410			410
1/4	Bal b/d	60			

Total amount owed by debtors = £1,530.

Purchase Ledger

Bee plc

25/3	CB	170	1/3	Bal b/d	170

Eff Ltd

7/3	CB	100	1/3	Bal b/d	240
25/3	CB	120	3/3	PDB	200
31/3	Bal c/d	220			
		440			440
			1/4	Bal b/d	220

Jay plc

7/3	CB	100	1/3	Bal b/d	290
31/3	Bal c/d	260	19/3	PDB	70
		360			360
			1/4	Bal b/d	260

Kay plc

25/3	CB	220	1/3	Bal b/d	160
31/3	Bal c/d	280	19/3	PDB	340
		500			500
			1/4	Bal b/d	280

Total amount owed to creditors = £760.

Nominal Ledger

Sales Ledger Control

1/3	Bal b/d	1,450	31/3	CB	1,070
31/3	SDB	1,150	31/3	Bal c/d	1,530
		2,600			2,600
1/4	Bal b/d	1,530			

Purchase Ledger Control

31/3	CB	710	1/3	Bal b/d	860
31/3	Bal c/d	760	31/3	PDB	610
		1,470			1,470
			1/4	Bal b/d	760

Bank

1/3	Bal b/d	3,400	31/3	Creditors	710
31/3	Debtors	1,070	31/3	Wages	2,420
31/3	Sales	480	31/3	Bal c/d	1,820
		4,950			4,950
1/4	Bal b/d	1,820			

The Journal

The vast majority of the entries to the nominal ledger will come from the cash book and the sales and purchase day books. There are, however, occasions when an entry must be made which is not routine in nature. The journal is used to ensure that such entries are recorded correctly.

Journal entries may have to be made in the following circumstances:

- to correct errors,
- to record the acquisition or disposal of fixed assets,
- to record or adjust provisions, such as the provision for bad debts or for corporation tax,
- to record the issue or redemption of shares or other financial instruments, and
- to make adjustments at the year end for items such as prepayments, accruals, depreciation, and closing stock.

Journal entries are laid out as follows:

Name of account to be debited   Amount
     Name of account to be credited   Amount
Narrative and reference to supporting vouchers.

This arrangement ensures that double entry is maintained. Without the journal, it would be possible to process only one-half of the adjustment. The journal also ensures that the reasons for any adjustment do not become forgotten. The company's auditors may query the need for an adjustment, especially if the reasons for it are not immediately obvious.

Progress Test 2

Draft journal entries for the following adjustments:

1.   Write off a bad debt which had been valued at £500.

2. Increase the provision for bad debts by £2,000.

3. Correct the misposting of £300 spent on a fixed asset to the repairs account.

4. Record the revaluation of an asset which is thought to be worth £18,000. This asset had originally cost £10,000 and had been depreciated by £2,000.

5. Adjust a provision for corporation tax from £3,500 to £3,300.

Solution to Progress Test 2

1. The asset of debtors has been reduced and the expense of bad debts increased.

   Debit   Bad debts   £500
      Credit   Debtors   £500

   Being bad debt written off.

2. Increasing a provision has the effect of either increasing a liability or reducing an asset and also increasing an expense or other charge against profit.

   Debit   Bad debts   £2,000
      Credit   Provision for Bad Debts   £2,000

   Being increase in provision for fixed assets.

3. Reduce an expense and increase an asset.

   Debit   Fixed Assets – Cost   £300
      Credit   Repairs   £300

   Being correction of misposting.

4. The figure for assets at cost or revaluation must be increased to £18,000 and the depreciation charged to date must be cancelled.

   Debit   Fixed Asset – Cost or Revaluation   £8,000
                  Fixed Asset – Depreciation   £2,000
      Credit   Revaluation   £10,000

   Being revaluation of fixed asset.

5.   Both the provision and the charge against profit must be reduced.

Debit   Taxation   £200
     Credit   Profit and Loss   £200

Being adjustment to provision for corporation tax.

The credit to the profit and loss account will appear in the form of an adjustment to the tax charge for the year.

Computerised systems

Bookkeeping is an obvious application for computers. Large amounts of data must be processed in accordance with a set of structured rules. Maintaining the system manually is labour-intensive, and therefore expensive. Manual systems are also inflexible in the sense that it can be difficult to extract summaries on an *ad hoc* basis. If, for example, it was necessary to know what percentage of outstanding sales invoices were overdue for payment, it would be very time-consuming to go through the sales ledger and analyse the ages of the various balances.

The nature of controls is different within a computerised accounting system. In most systems, the various files are integrated. If a purchase invoice is recorded in the file which is equivalent to the purchase day book in a manual system, the program will usually update both the purchases account and the purchase ledger control account in the nominal ledger and also the relevant creditors' account in the purchase ledger. Furthermore, the program will often generate a payment for the invoice, either by printing out a cheque or by making a payment through the bank's credit transfer system. This latter method involves the preparation of a magnetic tape which contains details of all of the payments which are to be made. This tape is then sent to the bank where it is used to transfer funds from the company's bank account to those of the payees.

The integration of programs and updating of files is necessary to prevent the need to key the same data into the computer more than once. It is also contrary to the concept of segregation of duties. If a fraudulent employee managed to input an invalid invoice into the system, he or she could be rewarded for his dishonesty by the automatic generation of a payment. Unlike human bookkeepers, computers cannot query their instructions or refuse to do something which appears to be dishonest.

The effects of computerisation on internal control are not all bad. Computers can be programmed to make comparisons which would not be cost-effective in a manual system. When processing wages payments, for example, a computer can be programmed to check that every employee on the payroll has a valid personnel file. This makes it much more difficult to commit the fairly simple fraud of inventing a bogus worker and stealing the extra pay packet. Computers can also replicate some of the manual controls. The program which processes purchase invoices can ensure that the goods were ordered and subsequently received by comparing details on invoices as they are processed with the relevant entries in the inventory files. Any mis-matches can be automatically rejected or queried. The computer's ability to process data quickly also permits a more detailed review of operations, an example of this being the aged analysis of debtors mentioned earlier, which can be generated easily and as a matter of routine for credit control purposes.

The fact that the computer keeps the accounting records and may also have control over certain assets if payments or transfers of stock are authorised electronically means that the system must be protected. Many frauds have been committed by dishonest staff and even by outsiders who have managed to gain access to files and changed either programs or data files. This protection must comprise both physical security and also restriction of access via remote terminals and other communication devices.

The nature of the computer system will have an effect on the type of protection which is required. Large mainframe computers may have been designed in such a way as to allow staff from other branches to communicate with the system using terminals linked to the telephone system. This creates an obvious security risk because outsiders may try to obtain unauthorised access. If the company employs its own programmers to write and update programs, then there will have to be a proper procedure to ensure that new programs are properly tested before becoming operational and also to ensure that any changes are reviewed before they are keyed in. Programming staff should not have direct access to the system itself because their skills would enable them to make fraudulent changes. Any alterations should be properly documented and input by the operating staff.

A company which relies on a microcomputer and which uses programs purchased from software houses will have a different set of problems. There is unlikely to be any means of remote access to the system and it would be difficult, if not impossible, to interfere with the programs. The fact that the machine is designed for use within an office, with no need for environmental protection or a special electricity supply, means that it is likely to be relatively easily accessible. This may make it possible for staff to make changes to data or enter fictitious transactions when the machine is not being used by the operator. It is extremely important that all files are protected by passwords and by other measures, such as data encryption.

Summary

Routine transactions are recorded and summarised in various day books. The totals from these records are entered into the nominal ledger in order to keep the account balances up to date.

There is usually only one account within the nominal ledger itself for each of the debtors and creditors. These 'control' accounts are supported by sales and purchase ledgers which contain accounts for each customer and supplier.

Duties should be allocated in such a way that the authorisation of a transaction, the custody of the related assets, and the recording of it are each the responsibility of different people. It becomes possible to conceal fraud if duties are not segregated in this way.

The computerisation of the accounting system makes it relatively easy to extract information for management and control purposes. It is also possible to extend the extent of cross-checking between files and records. The system must, however, be protected from attempts to interfere with program or data files.

7 Interpretation of financial statements

The whole point of preparing financial statements is that they should inform their users about the performance and the financial position of the business to which they relate. This chapter will look at the interpretation of financial statements, concentrating on the technique of ratio analysis. This material is important. The interpretation of accounting information is examined at virtually every level in all of the professional bodies' examinations, both in financial accounting papers and also in financial management. This material is also very useful in auditing papers.

Objectives

This chapter covers the following key issues:

- The calculation of accounting ratios (see progress tests 1 and 2)
- The analysis of company performance and financial position (see progress test 3)

Why calculate ratios?

The individual figures in a set of financial statements mean very little when taken on their own. It is not particularly helpful to be told that a company has made a profit of £1 million. This figure must be related to something else before it has any real meaning. If, for example, the company's shareholders have invested £10 million in the company then the profit represents a return of 10%. This is a more useful statistic because it can be compared with returns available from other investments.

A ratio is simply the relationship between two numbers. Some textbooks list a number of 'key' ratios and almost seem to imply that the interpretation of a set of financial statements can be described as a mechanical process of long division. Nothing could be further from the truth. There are many potentially useful ratios which are rarely described in books, any of which might yield a useful insight in an examination question. In any case, relatively few marks are awarded for the calculation of the ratios themselves. Most credit is awarded for the interpretation of the results obtained.

This chapter will describe a number of formulae. It is vitally important that you understand the reasoning behind each one. This is partly because it will be easier to remember them if you grasp their logic and partly because it will be very much easier to discuss the results obtained if you know what each formula represents.

Perspective

It is very difficult to interpret a set of statements unless you have been told why you are examining them. There are a number of possible scenarios:

- You might have been told to compare the quality of the management of two companies. This will require the use of ratios designed to measure profitability and efficiency.
- You might have been told to consider whether it is safe to make a loan to a company. This will require the calculation of ratios designed to measure solvency and the volatility of cash flows.
- You might have been told to imagine that you are the auditor of a company. This will usually require the calculation of ratios which are intended to highlight anomalies within figures which ought to be selected for more detailed testing.

Whenever a question tells you why you have been asked to interpret the financial statements of a company you should be careful to select the ratios which are most appropriate for your needs. If necessary, you should be prepared to use non-standard formulae which are more appropriate to the task in hand.

Illustration 1

The financial statements of Alpha Ltd are shown below.

Profit and Loss Account for the Year Ended 31 December 19X7

	£	£
Sales		500,000
Opening Stock	25,000	
Purchases	305,000	
Closing Stock	30,000	

	£	£
Cost of Sales		300,000
Gross Profit		200,000
Other Operating Expenses	60,000	
Interest	24,000	
		84,000
Net Profit		116,000
Dividend		20,000
		96,000
Profit brought forward		160,000
Profit carried forward		256,000

Balance Sheet as at 31 December 19X7

	£	£
Fixed Assets		540,000
Current Assets		
Stock	30,000	
Debtors	62,500	
Bank	7,000	
	99,500	
Current Liabilities		
Creditors	37,875	
Proposed Dividend	20,000	
	57,875	
Working Capital		41,625
		581,625
Long Term Liabilities		
Debenture Loans		200,000
		381,625
Share capital		125,625
Profit and Loss		256,000
		381,625

Ignore taxation.

We will use this set of financial statements to illustrate the calculation of the main accounting ratios, assuming that we wish to evaluate the performance of Alpha's management.

The main accounting ratios

There are four main groups of ratios:

1. Those which measure profitability.
2. Those which measure solvency.
3. Those which measure business efficiency.
4. Those which relate to the business's financial structure.

Profitability Ratios

The profitability ratios are used to check that the company is generating an acceptable return for its owners. A number of benchmarks can be used: previous years' figures, ratios calculated for similar businesses, industry averages, etc. Management should consider the reasons for any ratios which are poorer than expected to see whether they imply that performance could be improved.

Return on capital employed

Return on capital employed is the most important profitability ratio. It measures the relationship between the amount invested in the business and the returns generated for those investors.

The calculation of return on capital employed is complicated by the fact that capital employed can be measured in a number of different ways. It is vitally important that the figure for 'return' is calculated in a consistent manner with that for 'capital employed'.

The two main formulae for return on capital employed are:

$$\frac{\text{Net profit before tax and interest}}{\text{Share capital + Reserves + Long term debt}} \times 100$$

and

$$\frac{\text{Net profit before tax}}{\text{Share capital + Reserves}} \times 100$$

The first formula defines capital employed in terms of the total amount invested in the company, by both shareholders and lenders. In order to be consistent, the figure for return must show the total amount generated on behalf of these investors. That is why interest has been added back.

Alpha Ltd's return on capital employed would be:

$$\frac{116,000 + 24,000}{125,625 + 256,000 + 200,000} \times 100 = 24\%$$

Thus, Alpha's investors have invested a total of £581,625 in the company. A profit of £140,000 has been generated during the year, representing a return of 24%.

The second formula is sometimes called return on equity. It takes a rather narrower view of capital employed, restricting the definition to the investment made by the shareholders. Alpha Ltd's return on equity was:

$$\frac{116,000}{125,625 + 256,000} \times 100 = 30\%$$

The shareholders invested a total of £381,625 in the company. This investment yielded a profit of £116,000, representing a return of 30%.

The choice of formula depends on the reason for calculating return on capital employed. The first formula is most useful for measuring the overall effectiveness of the company's management. It can be used to compare the profitability of companies which use debt and equity in different proportions. The second formula is more useful when measuring profitability from the point of view of individual shareholders.

It is debatable whether profit should be taken before or after tax. It might be argued that each company is affected by tax in a different way. Some businesses have more opportunity to minimise their tax charge. It is, therefore, probably easier to compare profit before tax. Alternatively, it might be argued that it is part of management's responsibility to minimise the tax charge. In this case, it might be felt that profit after tax is a more appropriate measure of management's success. It can, therefore, be appropriate to take profit either before or after tax.

Return on capital employed differs from the other ratios in that it is always desirable for this percentage to be as high as possible. It is, however, difficult to decide whether the ratio is high enough. The level of return must be compared with the returns available from alternative investments and also with the level of risk undertaken. Alpha's return of 24% is certainly higher than the low-risk alternatives of investing in bank deposit accounts. It could, however, still be regarded as inadequate if it was less than the returns generated by similar businesses in the same industry or if Alpha was in a very high-risk sector.

Gross profit percentage

The gross profit percentage measures a company's ability to trade effectively. It is simply the ratio of gross profit to sales:

$$\frac{\text{Gross profit}}{\text{Sales}} \times 100$$

Alpha's gross profit percentage was:

$$\frac{200,000}{500,000} \times 100 = 40\%$$

Obviously, mark-ups will vary between industries. In general, it should be possible to compare the gross profit percentages of similar businesses. It can, however, be difficult to analyse any differences.

If, for the sake of argument, Alpha was being compared with a similar business which had a gross profit percentage of only 30%, you might draw the following conclusions:

- Alpha is better at extracting higher prices from its customers;
- Alpha is better at negotiating lower prices from its suppliers; or
- Alpha is overcharging for its products – and could be losing business as a result.

Clearly, it is impossible to tell which of these is the most likely explanation without obtaining further information. This is, in fact, a common problem when comparing ratios in examination questions. It might be possible to suggest reasons for differences between ratios. Sometimes, it will be impossible to tell which is the better set of results. The ratios can, however, be used to pinpoint areas which merit further investigation.

Net profit percentage

The net profit percentage is probably the least useful of the profitability ratios. It is simply:

$$\frac{\text{Net profit}}{\text{Sales}} \times 100$$

This ratio simply compares profit with one of many possible measures of the company's size, namely, turnover. It would be equally appropriate to compare net profit with the value of fixed assets, the number of employees, the square footage of the company's factory, or whatever.

Unlike the gross profit percentage, there is unlikely to be any point in comparing net profit percentages, even for companies in the same industry. The net profit figures might not be directly comparable because of differences in accounting policy. Even if these can be reconciled, the net profit percentages might differ because of differences in operating or financing policies. If one company has purchased its premises and another has rented them, then the net profit figures will differ because the depreciation charged by one business will not be the same as the amount paid by the other for rent. If one company relies heavily on borrowing and another is financed entirely by equity, then the former will have interest charges in its profit and loss account while the latter will not.

Alpha's net profit percentage is:

$$\frac{116,000}{500,000} \times 100 = 23\%$$

In general, it is better not to calculate the net profit percentage unless an examination question specifically asks you to do so. It might, however, be useful for monitoring the control of overheads over time. Any downward trend in the net profit percentage could imply that gross profit is falling. If the gross profit percentage suggests that this is not the case, then a fall in net profit percentage could be due to overhead costs rising faster than the growth in sales.

Liquidity ratios

While it is important for a business to be profitable, profit is not sufficient on its own to guarantee survival. There must be sufficient liquid assets available to ensure that short term commitments can be met, otherwise the company could be forced into liquidation.

Current ratio

The current ratio is simply the ratio of current assets to current liabilities:

$$\frac{\text{Current assets}}{\text{Current liabilities}}$$

Alpha's current ratio is:

$$\frac{99,500}{57,875} = 1.7{:}1$$

Notice that this figure is usually expressed as a ratio rather than as a percentage.

The current ratio is a measure of the company's ability to meet its short term debts. This is important because the company could run out of cash and be forced into liquidation even if it was making profits.

Working capital has to be managed very carefully. The company must invest enough money in working capital to enable it to conduct its business and meet its day-to-day obligations to suppliers and employees. It cannot, however, afford to invest too much in unproductive current assets. Doing so might leave the directors open to allegations of inefficiency. This could trigger off a takeover bid.

It is sometimes suggested that the 'optimal' current ratio is 2.0:1. Experience has shown that most businesses need current assets worth roughly twice current liabilities. More is usually regarded as excessive. This guideline must, however, be treated carefully. Some businesses do not need as high a current ratio, the classic example being a food retailer whose stocks are usually sold within days or even hours of them being put on the shelves and whose customers pay immediately in cash. Such a business could survive quite easily on a current ratio which is very much lower than 2.0:1. At the other extreme, a business which had erratic cash receipts might require a very much higher current ratio.

Alpha's current ratio seems rather low. It would, however, be worth looking at previous years' figures. If the company has always managed to survive on a ratio of 1.7:1 or thereabouts then there is probably little to worry about. Conversely, if the ratio is falling then this might indicate that the company is running into liquidity problems.

Quick assets ratio (Acid test ratio)

The quick assets ratio is a rather more stringent measure of liquidity than the current ratio. It is the ratio of 'quick' assets (i.e. excluding stock) to current liabilities:

$$\frac{\text{Current assets} - \text{Stock}}{\text{Current liabilities}}$$

Alpha's quick asset ratio is:

$$\frac{99,500 - 30,000}{57,875} = 1.2:1$$

By ignoring stock, the ratio concentrates on those current assets which are immediately available to pay the creditors as and when they fall due.

It is often suggested that the 'optimal' quick assets ratio is 1.0:1. Again, this is subject to the nature of the business. A retailer will survive quite happily on a ratio of only 0.3:1. Some businesses need a much higher ratio.

Alpha's ratio of 1.2:1 seems surprisingly high, given the doubts voiced earlier about the adequacy of the current ratio. It would appear that the company does not hold much in the way of stocks. This will tend to drive the current ratio down without having any adverse affect on the quick assets ratio.

Efficiency Ratios

The efficiency ratios are related to the liquidity ratios. They give an insight into the effectiveness of the company's management of the components of working capital.

Stock turnover

It is possible to calculate the average number of days taken by the business to sell a piece of stock:

$$\frac{\text{Stock}}{\text{Cost of sales}} \times 365$$

This is equivalent to taking the amount of stock held by the business, dividing by the rate at which stock is consumed in a year and multiplying by the number of days in a year. Alpha Ltd's stock turnover is:

$$\frac{30,000}{300,000} \times 365 = 37 \text{ days}$$

This means that, on average, any given piece of stock will spend 37 days 'on the shelf' before it is sold.

Obviously, it is desirable for this period to be as short as possible. The shorter the stock turnover period, the more quickly stock can be converted into cash. The stock turnover ratio can, however, be too short. It is easy to reduce the figure produced by this ratio; the company can simply allow its stocks to run down. This could, however, be counter-productive if it led to stoppages in production because there were inadequate stocks of materials or components. Similarly, holding inadequate stocks of finished goods could cost the company both trade and goodwill if it is unable to meet customer demand.

It is difficult to tell whether 37 days is 'good' or 'bad'. It would be helpful if Alpha could be compared with a similar company or if previous years' figures were available.

Sometimes this ratio is calculated using constants of 52 or 12 to express the turnover in terms of weeks or months. It is also possible to invert the formula and leave out the constant to show how often stock has 'turned over' during the year:

$$\frac{\text{Cost of sales}}{\text{Stock}} = \frac{300,000}{30,000} = 10 \text{ times}$$

Debtors turnover

This is a measure of the average length of time taken for debtors to settle their balance:

$$\frac{\text{Debtors}}{\text{Sales}} \times 365$$

Alpha's ratio is:

$$\frac{62,500}{500,000} \times 365 = 46 \text{ days}$$

Again, it is desirable for this ratio to be as short as possible. It will be better for the company's cash flow if debtors pay as quickly as possible. It can, however, be difficult to press for speedier payment. Doing so could damage the company's relationship with its suppliers.

In general, most businesses request payment within 30 days of the delivery of goods. Most customers tend to delay payment for some time beyond this. Alpha's ratio appears reasonable: debtors are not taking an unrealistic time to pay and there is nothing to suggest that Alpha is putting undue pressure on its customers.

If the company sells goods for cash and for credit then it is important to divide the debtors figure by credit sales only. If sales cannot be broken down then the ratio will be distorted. The classic case of this occurred when a student divided the sundry debtors of a supermarket chain by the turnover figure (virtually all of which was cash) and came to the conclusion that the debtors turnover ratio was approximately 0.007 days (about 10 minutes!).

Creditors turnover

This is the average time taken to pay creditors:

$$\frac{\text{Creditors}}{\text{Purchases}} \times 365$$

Alpha's creditor turnover was:

$$\frac{37,875}{305,000} \times 365 = 45 \text{ days}$$

While the company should collect cash from its customers as quickly as possible, it should try to delay making payments to its suppliers. Effectively, this is equivalent to taking out an interest-free loan which can be used to help finance working capital. Again, the company must use some restraint. If it becomes regarded as a slow payer then it might find it difficult to obtain credit. Indeed, there are credit-rating agencies which compile lists of companies which have poor reputations.

Alpha's ratio of approximately a month and a half seems reasonable.

Published accounts do not usually state the purchases figure. It is possible to obtain a crude estimate of the creditors turnover by using the cost of sales figure instead.

The working capital cycle

The efficiency ratios are related to those which measure solvency. The working capital cycle gives an indication of the length of time cash spends tied up in current assets.

This is calculated as follows:

Stock turnover + Debtors turnover – Creditors turnover

The logic behind this is that stock cannot be converted into cash until it has been sold and then the customer pays for the goods. This must be offset against the fact that no cash is actually invested until the company has paid the supplier for the goods. Thus, Alpha's working capital cycle is:

$$37 + 46 - 45 = 38 \text{ days}$$

This means that, on average, the company's money is tied up in any given piece of stock for 38 days before it is recovered (with profit).

Rounding

Notice that all of the ratios which are expressed in terms of percentages or a number of days have been rounded off to the nearest whole number. The other figures have been rounded off to the first decimal place. There is little point in providing more detailed figures. Indeed, there is so much subjectivity inherent in the preparation of the accounting statements on which the ratios are based that it would be misleading to produce more 'accurate' ratios.

Progress Test 1

Charlie Ltd and Bravo Ltd are both manufacturing companies in the same industry. Calculate the ratios described above for the two companies. Comment on the effectiveness of each company's management. (Hint: when calculating the liquidity ratios, think carefully about the treatment of the recoverable ACT.)

Profit and Loss Accounts for the Year Ended 30 June 19X7

	Bravo Ltd		Charlie Ltd	
	£	£	£	£
Sales		700,000		1,200,000
Cost of Sales		(420,000)		(660,000)
Gross Profit		280,000		540,000
Other Operating Expenses	(32,000)		(46,000)	
Interest	(60,000)		(24,000)	
		(92,000)		(70,000)
Net Profit for Year		188,000		470,000
Tax	(37,600)		(84,600)	
Dividend	(28,200)		(103,400)	
		(65,800)		(188,000)
		122,200		282,000
Retained Profit b/fwd		147,000		158,000
Retained Profit c/fwd		269,200		440,000

Balance Sheets as at 30 June 19X7

	Bravo Ltd		Charlie Ltd	
	£	£	£	£
Fixed Assets		900,000		1,513,000
Current Assets				
Stock	70,000		93,500	
Debtors	93,333		140,000	
Recoverable ACT	9,400		34,467	
Bank	87,000		78,000	
	259,733		345,967	
Current Liabilities				
Creditors	(45,500)		(140,000)	
Tax	(47,000)		(119,067)	
Proposed Dividend	(28,200)		(103,400)	
	(120,700)		(362,467)	
Working Capital		139,033		(16,500)
		1,039,033		1,496,500
Debentures		(500,000)		(200,000)
		539,033		1,296,500
Share Capital		269,833		856,500
Reserves		269,200		440,000
		539,033		1,296,500

Solution to Progress Test 1

	Bravo Ltd	Charlie Ltd
Return on capital employed	$\dfrac{188,000 + 60,000}{539,033 + 500,000} = 24\%$	$\dfrac{470,000 + 24,000}{1,296,500 + 200,000} = 33\%$
Gross profit percentage	$\dfrac{280,000}{700,000} = 40\%$	$\dfrac{540,000}{1,200,000} = 45\%$
Net profit percentage	$\dfrac{188,000}{700,000} = 27\%$	$\dfrac{470,000}{1,200,000} = 39\%$
Current ratio	$\dfrac{259,733 - 9,400}{120,700} = 2.1{:}1$	$\dfrac{345,967 - 34,467}{362,467} = 0.9{:}1$
Quick assets ratio	$\dfrac{259,733 - 9,400 - 70,000}{120,700} = 1.5{:}1$	$\dfrac{345,967 - 34,467 - 93,500}{362,467} = 0.6{:}1$

Stock turnover	$\dfrac{70,000}{420,000} \times 365 = 61$ days	$\dfrac{93,500}{660,000} \times 365 = 52$ days
Debtors turnover	$\dfrac{93,333}{700,000} \times 365 = 49$ days	$\dfrac{140,000}{1,200,000} \times 365 = 43$ days
Creditors turnover	$\dfrac{45,500}{420,000} \times 365 = 40$ days	$\dfrac{140,000}{660,000} \times 365 = 77$ days

Profitability

Charlie Ltd is obviously the more profitable company. The main reason for saying so is the much higher return on capital employed of 33% as opposed to Bravo's 24%.

Charlie's higher gross profit percentage has helped create these better returns, although it is worth pointing out that Bravo could be deliberately trying to undercut its competitors' prices. Another possibility is that Charlie's greater sales enable it to obtain higher discounts from its suppliers. If this is so then it is unfair to claim that the company is better managed than its smaller competitor.

Charlie's higher net profit percentage could indicate that overhead costs are better controlled than Bravo's, although it is possible that the ratio has been affected by accounting differences.

Liquidity

Bravo Ltd is the more liquid company with a current ratio approaching the (textbook) optimum of 2.0:1.

It is unlikely that a manufacturing company could continue to operate with a current ratio of only 0.9:1. It is likely that Charlie's management will have to look for additional finance to avoid running into difficulties in meeting their debts.

A company which is operating from an inadequate working capital base is said to be 'overtrading'. Typically, companies run into this problem because they try to expand too quickly. This appears to have happened to Charlie Ltd.

Activity ratios

At first glance, Charlie's ratios appear better than Bravo's. Stock and debtors are turning over more rapidly and the crude estimate of creditors turnover (using cost of sales as a surrogate for purchases) suggests that greater advantage is being taken of the credit facilities offered by suppliers. The discussion of liquidity could, however, put these figures in a different light. If Charlie is short of cash then it will only be natural for the company to try to collect payment from debtors as quickly as possible and to delay restocking for as long as possible. Indeed, the very long creditors turnover period could suggest that the company is unable to find the money with which to pay off its balance.

Notes

a.   Notice that the ratios were calculated and presented in tabular form before any comments were made. Doing so makes it easier to spot relationships between figures. It also provides practice for those questions where the examiner provides tables of ratios and gives marks only for comment.

b.   The ACT recoverable has not been included as a current asset for the purposes of the liquidity ratios because this balance will not be recovered until approximately 21 months after the year end.

c.   There is often scope for disagreement about the interpretation of ratios. It could be argued that Charlie's low liquidity ratios are indicative of aggressive treasury management. In practice the ratios would be used as a starting point and more information would be collected to confirm any suspicions raised.

Financial structure

The final series of ratios relate to the manner in which the company is financed.

Gearing

The manner in which a business is financed can have a marked effect on the risks associated with investing in or lending to it. A company which makes heavy use of borrowings is a riskier prospect than one which does not. This is partly because the increased borrowings increase the sheer amount of money which must be found every year in order to service the debt. Borrowing also has a slightly more subtle effect on the volatility of the shareholders' returns.

Every year, the company has to pay a fixed amount of interest on its borrowings. In relatively poor years, this charge could represent a comparatively significant proportion of the company's earnings before interest. This will leave very little profit for the shareholders. In extreme cases, a relatively small downturn in profits before interest could have a very serious effect on the shareholders' return. Suppose, for example, a company was financed by £2m of 12% debt and £2m of equity. Every year the company would have to pay £240,000 interest. If the average earnings before interest were, say, £540,000 then the shareholders' earnings before tax would amount to £300,000 giving them a return of 15% on their equity. If the company had a bad year and the earnings before interest were halved to £270,000 then the shareholders would be left with only £30,000, a return of only 1.5%. Thus, halving profit before interest would reduce the return by a factor of 10. Gearing can also affect returns in good years. If the company had a particularly good year, perhaps doubling its profit before interest to £1,080,000, then the lenders would still be entitled to only £240,000. This would leave £840,000 for the shareholders, representing a return of 42%. Thus, doubling profit before interest increases the shareholders' pre-tax returns by a factor of 2.8.

The proportion of debt to equity is called 'gearing' because of the way in which debt multiplies movement in the same manner as the mechanical gears work in a car. Gearing can be measured using the following formulae:

$$\frac{\text{Long term debt (including preference shares)}}{\text{Long term debt (including preference shares)} + \text{Equity}} \times 100$$

or

$$\frac{\text{Long term debt (including preference shares)}}{\text{Equity}} \times 100$$

The first formula measures debt as a proportion of total finance, while the second measures it as a proportion of equity. Thus, the two formulae give rather different answers. The first version of the formula is the more common.

Thus, Alpha Ltd's gearing ratio is $200,000/(200,000 + 381,625) = 34.4\%$.

Notice that preference capital is always treated as if it were debt rather than equity. This is because preference dividends usually have to be paid before any ordinary dividend can be recommended.

The 'acceptable' level of gearing varies according to the company's ability to provide security and the stability of its earnings and also according to the attitudes of lenders. In the UK a company whose gearing ratio (using the first of the formulae) had reached 40% would be considered highly geared. This varies from country to country. Japanese companies tend to borrow a great deal of their finance and so a gearing ratio of 40% would actually be considered quite low.

Bank overdrafts have to be treated with care when calculating gearing. Strictly, overdrafts are short term loans which are repayable on demand. Companies can, however, have overdrafts on an almost permanent basis. If an overdraft had fluctuated between, say, £50,000 and £75,000 for several years, it would be valid to treat £50,000 of the balance at the year end as part of long term debt for the purposes of this ratio.

Interest cover

The effects of gearing on the business's cash flows can also be measured using the interest cover ratio. This is simply the amount of profits before interest and tax divided by the interest charge for the year. Alpha's interest cover is £(200,000 - 60,000)/24,000 = 5.8 times. This means that profit before interest and tax would have to be reduced by a factor of 5.8 before interest charges would be sufficient to force it into a loss-making situation.

Progress Test 2

Calculate gearing and interest cover ratios for Bravo Ltd and Charlie Ltd.

Solution to Progress Test 2

	Bravo Ltd	Charlie Ltd
Gearing	$\dfrac{500,000}{539,033 + 500,000} = 48\%$	$\dfrac{200,000}{1,296,500 + 200,000} = 13\%$
Interest cover	$\dfrac{188,000 + 60,000}{60,000} = 4$ times	$\dfrac{470,000 + 24,000}{24,000} = 21$ times

Charlie Ltd has a very low gearing ratio and its interest cover is extremely high. If the company is faced with liquidity problems then it should not have any trouble in finding a lender. Bravo, on the other hand, seems to be at the limit of its borrowing capacity with high gearing and interest cover of only four times.

Progress Test 3

Echo plc is a holding company with several subsidiaries, all of which are involved in the manufacture of domestic electrical appliances. You have been asked to evaluate the performance of the managements of Foxtrot Ltd and Golf Ltd, two companies belonging to the Echo group. Examine the financial statements given below and compare the manner in which each company is being run.

Profit and Loss Accounts for the Year Ended 31 December 19X4

	Foxtrot Ltd		Golf Ltd	
	£000	£000	£000	£000
Sales		1,000		2,200
Cost of Sales		(400)		(1,430)
Gross Profit		600		770
Selling and Distribution	(110)		(150)	
Administration	(170)		(180)	
Interest	(12)		(18)	
		292		348
Net Profit for Year		308		422
Taxation		(78)		(76)
		230		346
Retained Profit b/f		450		620
Retained Profit c/f		680		966

Balance Sheets as at 31 December 19X4

	Foxtrot Ltd		Golf Ltd	
	£000	£000	£000	£000
Fixed Assets		851		1,200
Current Assets				
Stock	83		143	
Debtors	175		275	
Bank	27		17	
	285		435	
Current Liabilities				
Creditors	(40)		(191)	
Taxation	(78)		(76)	
	118		267	
Working Capital		167		168
		1,018		1,368
Debentures		(100)		(150)
		918		1,218
Share Capital		238		252
Reserves		680		966
		918		1,218

Solution to Progress Test 3

	Foxtrot Ltd	Golf Ltd
Return on capital employed	$\dfrac{308 + 12}{918 + 100} = 31\%$	$\dfrac{422 + 18}{1,218 + 150} = 32\%$
Gross profit percentage	$\dfrac{600}{1,000} = 60\%$	$\dfrac{770}{2,200} = 35\%$
Net profit percentage	$\dfrac{308}{1,000} = 31\%$	$\dfrac{422}{2,200} = 19\%$
Current ratio	$\dfrac{285}{118} = 2.4{:}1$	$\dfrac{435}{267} = 1.6{:}1$
Quick assets ratio	$\dfrac{285 - 83}{118} = 1.7{:}1$	$\dfrac{435 - 143}{267} = 1.1{:}1$
Stock turnover	$\dfrac{83}{400} \times 365 = 76$ days	$\dfrac{143}{1,430} \times 365 = 37$ days
Debtors turnover	$\dfrac{175}{1,000} \times 365 = 64$ days	$\dfrac{275}{2,200} \times 365 = 46$ days
Creditors turnover	$\dfrac{40}{400} \times 365 = 37$ days	$\dfrac{191}{1,430} \times 365 = 49$ days
Gearing	$\dfrac{100}{918 + 100} = 10\%$	$\dfrac{150}{1,218 + 150} = 11\%$
Interest cover	$\dfrac{308 + 12}{12} = 27$ times	$\dfrac{422 + 18}{18} = 24$ times

Profitability

The two companies have virtually the same return on capital employed. Golf would, however, appear to be better managed. It seems to have achieved a much higher turnover by adding a lower margin to its prices. It also appears to have controlled its overheads more effectively because the absolute amounts are not much greater than those of Foxtrot, despite the much higher sales activity.

It would, therefore, be possible for Foxtrot to increase its profits by introducing some of the policies implemented by Golf. This would boost its return on capital employed.

Liquidity

Neither company appears to be suffering any liquidity problems. Golf's current ratio appears slightly low. This is not, however, a matter to cause any real concern because the quick assets ratio is reasonably high. It looks as if Golf has managed to keep its stocks turning over rapidly.

Activity ratios

Golf appears to be turning its stocks over more quickly than Foxtrot. This is consistent with the suggestion that Golf is pricing its products more competitively.

Foxtrot's debtors ratio appears to be out of control. Perhaps customers are unwilling to pay its prices unless they are given liberal credit terms.

Foxtrot appears to be paying its creditors more quickly than it needs to. Golf's ratio is much more reasonable.

Financial structure

Neither company appears over-geared. Indeed, both have substantial unused borrowing capacity.

Some limitations of ratio analysis

Ratio analysis is a very useful technique for the interpretation of financial statements. It does, however, have its limitations. Some of these are outlined below.

- It diverts attention from the figures and statements themselves. It is important to look at aspects such as the sheer size of the company under consideration. A larger company will have more bargaining power and may be able to enjoy economies of scale. It is also important to look at information in the notes which is not usually reflected in the ratios. If someone is suing the company for damages this will be disclosed in a note stating the amount claimed and possibly giving an indication of the expected outcome. There will not be any mention of the matter in the balance sheet itself.
- Comparisons can be affected by different accounting policies or by other external factors. If, for example, two haulage companies use different methods for the calculation of depreciation, then any ratios based on their financial statements might not be comparable.

Similarly, two similar business could be affected to different extents by currency movements. A vehicle distributor selling Japanese cars will be exposed to movements in the value of Yen to a much greater extent than a distributor of British cars.

● There could be peculiarities of the trade which make it difficult to interpret certain ratios. A property company, say, might appear to have a very low return on capital employed. One reason for this is that the value of the properties shown in the balance sheet will be updated on a regular basis, thus increasing capital employed. This will make it difficult to compare results with a business whose assets have not been revalued.

Ratio analysis and the auditor

The auditor is appointed by the shareholders to express an opinion on whether the financial statements prepared by the directors give a true and fair view. The auditor's report gives some assurance that the financial statements are a credible source of information for decision making purposes. The auditor must collect evidence to support his or her opinion on the financial statements.

Auditors make very heavy use of ratio analysis. It can be used to identify anomalies in the figures themselves or to decide whether the financial statements do, in fact, give a true and fair view.

Anomalies

Almost every one of the 'key' ratios mentioned above can be used to spot possible anomalies within the figures. If, for example, the gross profit percentage figure has fallen dramatically, then the auditor will have to consider whether this could indicate that sales have been omitted from the sales account or that the cost of sales have been overstated, perhaps because of errors in the counting of closing stock.

If the auditor discovers an anomaly in the financial statements then he or she must investigate further to establish whether there has been any abuse. This is complicated by the fact that there may well be a perfectly innocent explanation for the variation in the ratio. The gross profit percentage could have fallen because of a price rise in raw materials or because of a change in pricing policy.

The activity ratios can be particularly useful in spotting anomalies. The auditor would be suspicious of increases in the time taken to sell stock or collect debtors' balances as measured by the stock and debtors turnover ratios. Any lengthening of these periods could indicate that the company is not writing off obsolete stocks or uncollectable debts. This will increase the average turnover figures. Again, such a change does not necessarily mean that the figures have been distorted. There are some even more obvious ratios which could be calculated for this purpose, none of which has been mentioned specifically above.

Changes in expenses can be compared with the general rate of inflation or the company's level of activity, as measured by turnover, to see whether or not they appear credible. The total cost of wages could be divided by the number of employees and any change since the previous year compared with the level of known pay awards. A downturn could be just as suspicious as an increase. If, for example, the cost of wages is significantly less than expected, it is possible that there has been a material understatement, perhaps of the year end accrual.

Truth and fairness

The auditor can make use of ratio analysis in forming an opinion on the truth and fairness of the financial statements themselves. It would, for example, be worth calculating the current ratio and the quick assets ratio to make sure that the company did not have any serious liquidity problems. If it had, then the auditor would have to consider whether the company could still be considered a going concern.

Other ratios can give an insight into management's motives when preparing the financial statements. If, for example, the return on capital employed ratios calculated from management accounts prepared during the year suggest that the company has had a poor year then the auditor should be alert to the possibility that the directors will try to overstate profits. This might be indicated by an upturn in return in capital employed when calculated using the draft annual accounts.

Summary

A ratio is simply the result obtained from dividing one figure by another. There are a number of 'key' accounting ratios which can be used to measure profitability, liquidity, the efficiency of working capital management and financial structure. These should, however, be supplemented as necessary by other ratios which are appropriate to the purpose of the investigation or the requirements of an examination question.

Ratio analysis should be regarded as a tool which helps when interpreting financial statements. It does, however, have its limitations. In general, these can be overcome by the use of common sense in considering the nature of the business and its accounting policies and by reading the information in the notes to the accounts.

Auditors often use ratios to identify figures which appear anomalous and require a more detailed investigation, to evaluate the risk of the company collapsing and to get an insight into the directors' motives.

8 The cash flow statement

Objectives

This chapter covers the following key topics:

- The difference between cash flows and profit, and the reconciliation of the two (see progress test 1)
- The preparation of the cash flow statement in accordance with the requirements of FRS 1 (see progress test 2)
- The derivation of a profit and loss account and balance sheet from the cash flow statement (see progress test 3)

Financial Reporting Standard 1

The cash flow statement is intended to supplement the profit and loss account and balance sheet. It identifies the inflows and outflows of cash to and from the company. This is important because cash is absolutely crucial to any business's survival.

The requirement to prepare a cash flow statement was laid down by FRS 1, the first standard to be produced by the Accounting Standards Board. This document was published in 1991 and came into effect immediately, although its application was not mandatory for financial statements relating to accounting periods ending before 23 March 1992.

FRS 1 replaced SSAP 10, which required the publication of a statement of source and application of funds. The earlier statements have been a popular source of examination questions. The introduction of the new FRS should make this area even more topical. This is not, however, a problem because the statements are not difficult to prepare provided a methodical approach is taken.

The purpose of the statement

The profit and loss account and balance sheet are useful statements in their own right. They do not, however, provide a sufficient insight into movements in cash balances. This is unfortunate because even profitable companies will collapse if they are not sufficiently liquid. Very few businesses could survive a prolonged cash outflow.

The profit figure for the year is unlikely to bear any resemblance to the increase or decrease in the company's bank balance over that period. Several entries in the profit and loss account, such as depreciation, do not involve cash. Furthermore, the profit and loss account recognises credit sales and purchases before any cash changes hands. Conversely, many receipts and payments, such as the proceeds of share issues and loan repayments, have no immediate impact on profit. It is possible for a company to trade profitably and still run into liquidity problems.

The bank balance is, of course, disclosed in the balance sheet. It is easy to see whether the balance has changed since the end of the previous year. It is, however, difficult to identify the major causes of such changes. Shareholders and other readers require a more structured description of the cash flows.

The cash flow statement is intended to answer the following types of question:

1. Why has the bank overdraft increased, despite the company having had a profitable year?
2. Is the company capable of generating cash, as opposed to profit, from its trading activities?
3. What was done with the loan which was taken out during the year?

The form and content of the statement

FRS 1 is designed to make it as easy as possible to compare the cash flow statements produced by different companies. Companies are required to list their cash flows, analysed into five main categories:

1. operating activities,
2. returns on investments and servicing of finance,
3. taxation,
4. investing activities, and
5. financing.

These headings must be used (and in the above order) unless, in extreme circumstances, there are very good reasons for adopting a different approach.

Illustration 1

The following set of financial statements will be used to illustrate the preparation of a cash flow statement.

ABC Ltd Profit and Loss Account for the Year Ended 31 December 19X3

	£000	£000
Sales		100
Opening Stock	8	
Purchases	50	
	58	
Closing Stock	17	
Cost of Goods Sold		41
Gross Profit		59
Wages	16	
Depreciation	14	
		30
Operating Profit		29
Interest		4
Net Profit		25
Taxation		8
		17
Dividend		7
		10
Balance Brought Forward		40
Balance Carried Forward		50

ABC Ltd Balance Sheets

	31 December 19X3			31 December 19X2		
	£000	£000	£000	£000	£000	£000
Fixed Assets						
Cost			200			180
Depreciation			92			78
			108			102

	31 December 19X3			31 December 19X2		
	£000	£000	£000	£000	£000	£000
Current Assets						
Stock		17			8	
Debtors		14			6	
Bank		3			7	
		34			21	
Current Liabilities						
Creditors	(13)			(5)		
Tax	(8)			(7)		
Dividend	(3)			(2)		
		(24)			(14)	
Net Current Assets			10			7
			118			109
Loan			(18)			(29)
			100			80
Share Capital			50			40
Profit and Loss			50			40
			100			80

These statements help demonstrate the need for the cash flow statement. The company has traded profitably, but has less in the bank at the end of the year than it had at the beginning. There are some obvious reasons for this: ABC Ltd has invested in new fixed assets, it has repaid part of its loan, and it has offset these outflows by means of an issue of shares. It would, however, help to have these movements disclosed clearly and concisely in a simple statement.

The figures in ABC Ltd's profit and loss account and balance sheet can be rearranged to give the following statement.

ABC Ltd Cash Flow Statement for the Year Ended 31 December 19X3

	£000	£000
Net inflow from operating activities		34
Returns on investment and servicing of finance		
Interest paid	(4)	
Dividends paid	(6)	
Net cash outflow from returns on investments and servicing of finance		(10)

	£000	£000
Taxation		
Corporation tax paid		(7)
Investing activities		
Payments to acquire tangible fixed assets		(20)
Net cash outflow before financing		(3)
Financing		
Repayment of loan	(11)	
Issue of ordinary share capital	10	
Net cash outflow from financing		(1)
Decrease in cash and cash equivalents		(4)

This statement shows how cash has been generated from trading activities and other sources. It also shows how these receipts have been applied. This gives a much clearer insight into ABC Ltd's cash flows.

Some of the headings have been broken down into sub-totals where it has been felt that this would help the reader. FRS 1 requires a total for each heading and a grand total showing the net cash inflow before financing. The manner in which these figures have been arrived at, and the notes which must accompany the cash flow statement, are described below.

Cash flows from operating activities

Cash flows from operations arise from the company's trading activities. They consist of receipts and payments of cash from sales, purchases and other activities. The figures in the profit and loss account have to be adjusted to allow for the fact that many transactions are on credit terms and there is usually a delay between the completion of a sale or a purchase and the related cash payment.

FRS 1 requires a note which shows how the figure for cash flows from operations has been arrived at. This can be laid out in either of two ways: (a) the 'direct' approach and (b) the 'indirect'. These arrive at the same total, but each does so in a different manner.

The direct approach lists the transactions in the profit and loss account which involved cash. Entries which did not affect the cash flows, such as depreciation, are ignored.

ABC Ltd's cash balances were affected by sales and purchases and by the payment of wages. The figures for sales and purchases have to be adjusted for movements in the debtors' and creditors' balances to arrive at the amounts actually received and paid during the year. The receipts and payments are, therefore, as follows.

Debtors

Bal b/d	6	Bank*	92
Sales	100	Bal c/d	14
	106		106
Bal b/d	14		

* Balancing figure

Similarly, payments to creditors were:

Creditors

Bank *	42	Bal b/d	5
Bal c/d	13	Purchases	50
	55		55
		Bal b/d	13

* Balancing figure

There was also a payment of £16,000 for wages.

Cash flows from operations would be calculated as follows under the direct method.

	£000
Receipts from debtors	92
Payments to suppliers	(42)
Payments to employees	(16)
Net cash inflow from operating activities	34

The indirect method starts with the operating profit and adjusts this to cancel any entries which had no effect on the bank balance. In most cases, these adjustments will be in respect of depreciation, any gains or losses on the disposal of fixed assets and any movements on the debtors', creditors' or stock balances.

ABC Ltd's reconciliation would appear as follows under the indirect method.

	£000
Operating profit	29
Depreciation charge	14
Increase in stock	(9)
Increase in debtors	(8)
Increase in creditors	8
Net cash inflow from operating activities	34

The sales figure in the profit and loss account must be adjusted for any increase or decrease in debtors. The addition of any decrease or subtraction of any increase gives the amount actually received from debtors during the period.

The cost of goods sold must be adjusted for any movements in stock and creditors. Adding any increase in stocks (or subtracting any decrease) will adjust the cost of sales figure to give the figure for purchases. Subtracting any increase in creditors (or adding any decrease) will then give the amount of cash actually paid during the year.

The two approaches are equivalent in that they give the same answer. The direct approach highlights the actual amounts received and paid from the various trading activities. This information could be valuable to anyone who wanted an insight into the company's cash flows. Such detailed information could, however, be regarded as commercially sensitive and so the FRS does not require the publication of the information derived from the direct approach. The indirect approach highlights differences between operating profit and operating cash flows and this could be useful to, say, an analyst who had prepared a forecast profit and loss account and who wanted to base a cash flow forecast on it.

FRS 1 requires a note which reconciles the operating profit to the cash flows from operations. Effectively, this means that the company must publish the figures calculated using the indirect approach. This does not, however, prevent the publication of the figures from the direct approach as a supplement if the directors feel that the benefits to be had from the additional disclosure outweigh the costs involved.

Notice that the figures are shown net of VAT. FRS 1 accepts that VAT has an effect on cash flows but still requires receipts and payments to be shown net. This is partly because VAT only has a short term effect on the timing of cash flows and partly because the inclusion of VAT could affect the allocation of cash flows to the standard headings. Any increase or decrease in the amount owed to the Customs and Excise should be allocated to cash flows from operating activities.

Progress Test 1

CDE plc Profit and Loss Account for the Year Ended
31 December 19X7

	£000
Turnover	74
Operating Expenses, less Other Operating Income	(55)
Operating Profit	19
Taxation	(7)
Profit after Taxation	12
Dividends	(8)
Profit Retained for Year	4
Retained Profits brought forward	22
Retained Profits carried forward	26

The following operating expenses were incurred during the year.

	£000
Wages	12
Auditor's Remuneration	2
Depreciation	14
Materials	37
Gas and Electricity	6
Gain on Sale of Asset	(4)
Government Grant	(9)
Rental Income	(3)
	55

In 19X5, the company received a government grant of £45,000 to assist in the development of a new product. It was expected that the product would take five years to develop and it was decided that the grant should be credited to a deferred income account and offset against operating expenses in five equal instalments.

The following figures were extracted from CDE plc's balance sheets.

	31 December 19X7 £000	31 December 19X6 £000
Stock	7	4
Debtors	8	7
Creditors	(5)	(3)

Calculate the cash flows from operations using both the direct and the indirect methods.

Solution to Progress Test 1

Direct Method

Debtors

Bal b/d	7	Bank *	73
Sales	74	Bal c/d	8
	81		81

* Balancing figure

The amount paid to creditors cannot be calculated without knowing the purchases figure. This can be derived by putting the opening and closing stock figures along with the cost of materials consumed into a 'T' account and taking the balancing figure.

Cost of goods sold

Bal b/d (stock)	4	Profit and Loss	37
Purchases *	40	Bal c/d	7
	44		44
Bal b/d	7		

* Balancing figure

Creditors

Bank *	38	Bal b/d	3
Bal c/d	5	Purchases	40
	43		43
		Bal b/d	5

* Balancing figure

	£000
Receipts from Customers	73
Rental Income	3
Payments to Suppliers	(38)
Wages	(12)
Auditor's Remuneration	(2)
Gas and Electricity	(6)
Net Inflow from Operations	18

Indirect Method

	£000
Operating Profit	19
Depreciation	14
Gain on Disposal of Assets	(4)
Grant	(9)
Increase in Debtors	(1)
Increase in Stock	(3)
Increase in Creditors	2
	18

Returns on investments and servicing of finance

This section of the statement shows cash flows in respect of the company's investment income and also any payments made to providers of finance, including both debt and equity.

Cash flows should be calculated in terms of amounts actually received and paid. Thus, any dividends received should be shown net of any related tax credits.

ABC Ltd has suffered a net outflow of £10,000 due to the servicing of finance.

Taxation

This section of the statement will deal only with taxes on revenue and capital profits. Any receipts or payments in respect of VAT should be dealt with as mentioned above in the section on cash flows from operating activities.

It was shown in Chapter 4 that there could be several balances in respect of taxation and that the charge for tax could include a number of components. Some of the adjustments involving taxation will have no effect on cash.

The simplest means of calculating the amount of tax paid is to use a 'T' account for taxation. All of the opening and closing balances should be entered into this account, including balances in respect of ACT and deferred tax. The total amount charged in the profit and loss account should also be entered, regardless of the adjustments which have been included in the tax charge. The balancing figure on this account should be the amount paid during the year.

The amount paid by ABC Ltd was calculated as follows.

Taxation

Bank *	7	Bal b/d		7
Bal c/d	8	Profit and Loss		8
	15			15
		Bal b/d		8

* Balancing figure

This is, of course, a rather simple example.

Illustration 2

The following balances appeared in the balance sheets of DEF plc.

	31 December 19X4 £000	31 December 19X3 £000
Current Liabilities		
Corporation Tax	200	190
ACT	20	13
Provisions for Liabilities		
Deferred Tax, less		
Recoverable ACT	400	370

The tax charge for 19X4 was calculated as follows.

	£000
Estimate for Year	220
Irrecoverable Tax Credits on FII	7
ACT Written off	14
Increase in Deferred Tax	30
	271
Over-provision from Previous Year	(10)
	261

The amount of tax paid during 19X4 can be derived from the following account.

Taxation

		Corporation Tax b/d	190
		ACT b/d	13
		Deferred Tax b/d	370
		Charge for Year	261
Bank *	214		
Corporation Tax b/d	200		
ACT b/d	20		
Deferred Tax b/d	400		
	834		834

* Balancing figure

Thus, a total of £214,000 was actually paid to the Inland Revenue during the year. This is the amount which should appear as an application in the company's statement of source and application of funds.

Investing activities

This section of the cash flow statement deals with those cash flows from investments in or disposals of fixed assets or of investments held as current assets.

Most businesses will have had some sales and purchases of fixed assets in the course of the year, and so it is necessary to take extra care with this section of the balance sheet. When calculating the funds generated from operations under the indirect method, it is necessary to add the depreciation charge back to the profit before tax because no actual movement of funds will have taken place as a result of this expense. Similarly, any loss on the disposal of a fixed asset will have to be added back because this is really no more than an adjustment to the depreciation charged during the life of the asset.

Acquisitions and disposals of fixed assets will lead to payments or receipts of cash. Any amount paid for new assets should be shown as an application. The proceeds from the disposal of a fixed asset should be shown as a source. The statement will be much clearer if these flows are shown separately rather than being netted off against one another.

Revaluations of assets will not affect the company's bank balance and so the effects of any such adjustment will have to be identified and kept separate from any increases or decreases arising from acquisitions or disposals.

Financing

The final section of the cash flow statement deals with amounts raised from the issue of shares or borrowing, and with any repayments of finance. This section deals exclusively with transactions involving principal, all payments of interest and dividends are dealt with under the heading of 'returns on investment and servicing of finance'.

If new shares have been issued during the year, it is important to consider exactly how much has been raised as a result. If the shares have been issued at a premium, then the amount by which the share premium account balance has risen will also have to be included as a source of finance.

Another possibility is that a 'bonus' issue of shares could have been made during the year. This involves giving each shareholder a number of new, fully paid shares. Normally, the number of shares received is in direct proportion to the number of shares held just before the issue. The shares are 'paid for' by debiting the profit and loss account, or some other reserve, with the nominal value of the shares issued. It is debatable whether such an issue will have any real effect on the wealth of either the company or its shareholders, but it will certainly have no effect on the company's funds and should be disregarded when drafting the statement of source and application of funds.

The items shown in the financing section of the statement must be reconciled to the figures in the opening and closing balance sheets.

Reconciliation with balance sheet figures

The net inflow or outflow of cash for the year must be reconciled to the related amounts in the opening and closing balance sheets for the period. Cash balances include 'cash equivalents' which are defined as:

> Short-term, highly liquid investments which are readily convertible into known amounts of cash without notice and which were within three months of maturity when acquired; less advances from banks repayable within three months from the date of the advance.

Notice that the three-month cut-off relates to the time of maturity or repayment when the asset of liability was acquired or incurred. Thus, a long term liability which was due to be repaid within three months would be excluded because of the length of its original term. This is not as illogical as it seems. The alternative would involve showing an inflow or outflow of cash in the main statement whenever a balance came within three months of maturity or repayment, even though no cash flow had actually occurred.

Thus, cash equivalents would include such items as balances in bank deposit accounts and overdrafts. Investments in quoted securities would be excluded, even if the company intended to resell them within three months, because their value can fluctuate rapidly.

Exceptional and extraordinary items

Cash flows from exceptional and extraordinary items should be shown separately under their relevant headings.

Interpreting the statement

The cash flow statement does not give enough information on its own to enable a reader to tell whether a company's funds have been well managed. An inflow of cash is not always desirable. A company which has excessive reserves of cash might find it advisable to run these down, perhaps by means of investment in fixed assets or even by means of a substantial dividend payment.

The effects of any net movement can only be measured by looking at the closing balance sheet and considering whether the relationships between the various components of working capital and long term finance are acceptable.

Even if a net inflow was necessary, the statement cannot show whether the most appropriate type of finance has been raised or whether it has been obtained from the cheapest source.

Progress Test 2

Prepare a cash flow statement for EFG plc for the year ended 31 December 19X7.

EFG plc Profit and Loss Account for the Year Ended
31 December 19X7

	Notes	£000	£000
Turnover			100
Cost of Sales			(46)
Gross Profit			54
Distribution Costs		(12)	
Administrative Expenses		(11)	
Other Operating Income		3	
			(20)
Operating Profit	[1]		34
Interest Payable			(2)
Profit on Ordinary Activities			32
Tax on Profit on			
Ordinary Activities			(8)
Profit on Ordinary Activities			
after Taxation			24
Extraordinary Items	[2]		(9)
Profit for the Financial Year			15
Dividends			(5)
Profit Retained for the Year			10
Retained Profits b/f			11
			21
Profits Capitalised on Bonus Issue	[9]		(2)
Retained Profits c/f			19

EFG plc Balance Sheets

	Notes	31 December 19X7 £000	31 December 19X7 £000	31 December 19X6 £000	31 December 19X6 £000
Fixed Assets					
Intangible Assets	[3]		12		17
Tangible Assets	[4]		28		16
			40		33
Current Assets					
Stocks		22		20	
Debtors		19		17	
Short term investments	[5]	3		2	
Cash at Bank		–		2	
		44		41	

	Notes	£000	£000	£000	£000
Creditors: Amounts falling due within one year	[6]	(29)		(21)	
Net Current Assets			15		20
Total Assets, less Current Liabilities			55		53
Creditors: Amounts falling due after more than one year	[7]		–		(20)
			55		33
Provisions for Liabilities and Charges	[8]		(3)		(8)
			52		25
Capital and Reserves					
Share Capital	[9]		20		10
Share Premium			10		4
Revaluation Reserve			3		–
Profit and Loss Account			19		11
			52		25

Notes

1. Operating Profit
    Operating profit is arrived at after charging the following :

	£000
Wages	11
Depreciation	9
Loss on Disposal	3
Auditor's Remuneration	2
Research and Development	
Current Expenditure	7
Amortisation of Deferred Expenditure	5

2. Extraordinary Items

	£000
Closure Costs	15
Tax Relief thereon	(6)
	9

3. Intangible Fixed Assets
    Deferred Development Costs

	£000
At 1/1/X7	17
Amortised	(5)
At 31/1/X7	12

4. Tangible Fixed Assets

	Land and Buildings £000	Plant and Machinery £000	Total £000
Cost or Valuation			
At 1/1/X7	9	21	30
Acquisitions	–	22	22
Disposals	–	(8)	(8)
Adjustment on Revaluation	1	–	1
At 31/12/X7	10	35	45
Depreciation			
At 1/1/X7	1	13	14
Disposals	–	(4)	(4)
Charge for Year	1	8	9
Adjustment on Revaluation	(2)	–	(2)
At 31/12/X7	–	17	17
Net Book Value			
At 31/12/X7	10	18	28
At 1/1/X7	8	8	16

5. Short term investments
Short term investments consist of government securities which were purchased within two months of their date of maturity.

6. Creditors: Amounts due within one year

	19X7 £000	19X6 £000
Bank Overdraft	1	–
Trade Creditors	16	15
Taxation	9	4
Dividends	3	2
	29	21

7. Creditors: Amounts due after one year

	19X7 £000	19X6 £000
Debentures	–	20

8.   Provisions for Liabilities and Charges

	19X7	19X6
	£000	£000
Deferred Taxation	3	8

9.   Share Capital
The company's shares have a nominal value of £1 each.
A bonus issue took place during the year. The shareholders received one fully paid share for every five previously held.
8,000 new shares were issued for cash.

Solution to Progress Test 2

EFG plc Cash Flow Statement for the Year Ended 31 December 19X7

	£000	£000
Net cash inflow from operating activities		33
Servicing of finance		
Interest paid	(2)	
Dividends paid	(4)	
Net cash outflow from servicing of finance		(6)
Taxation		
Corporation tax paid	(2)	
Tax paid		(2)
Investing activities		
Payments to acquire tangible fixed assets	(22)	
Receipts from sales of tangible fixed assets	1	
Net cash outflow from investing activities		(21)
Net cash inflow before financing		4
Financing		
Issue of ordinary share capital	14	
Repayment of debenture loan	(20)	
Net cash outflow from financing		(6)
Decrease in cash and cash equivalents		(2)

Notes to the cash flow statement

1. Reconciliation of operating profit to net cash inflow from operating activities

	£000
Operating profit	34
Depreciation	9
Loss on disposal of tangible fixed assets	3
Amortisation of research and development	5
Increase in stocks	(2)
Increase in debtors	(2)
Increase in creditors	1
Net cash inflow from continuing activities	48
Cash outflow from discontinuation	(15)
Net cash inflow from operating activities	33

2. Analysis of changes in cash and cash equivalents during the year

	£000
Balance at 31 December 19X6	4
Net cash outflow	(2)
Balance at 31 December 19X7	2

3. Analysis of the balances of cash and cash equivalents during the year

	19X7	19X6	Change in year
	£000	£000	£000
Cash at bank and in hand	–	2	(2)
Short term investments	3	2	1
Bank overdraft	(1)	–	(1)
	2	4	(2)

4. Analysis of changes in financing during the year

	Share capital	Share premium	Debenture loan
	£000	£000	£000
Balance at 31 December 19X6	10	4	20
Cash inflow/(outflow) from financing	8	6	(20)
Increase in share capital from bonus issue	2	–	–
	20	10	–

Workings

All figures in £000s

* Balancing figure

Dividends

Bank *	4	Bal b/d	2
Bal c/d	3	Profit and Loss	5
	7		7

Taxation

Bank *	2	Bal b/d – CT	4
Bal c/d – CT	9	Bal b/d – DT	8
Bal c/d – DT	3	Profit and Loss	2
	14		14

The charge for the year comprises the tax on profits on ordinary activities of £8,000 minus the tax relief on the extraordinary expense of £6,000 to leave a net charge of £2,000.

Disposal of fixed asset

Cost	8	Depreciation	4
		Profit and Loss (loss)	3
		Bank *	1
	8		8

Shares
The share capital has increased by £10,000 and the share premium by £6,000. £2,000 of this increase is due to the bonus issue and can, therefore, be ignored. This means that funds of £14,000 have been raised from the sale of shares.

A variation on the basic question

Examiners often attempt to test candidates' understanding by taking a 'standard' question and presenting it in a different way. It would, for example, be possible to provide a balance sheet as at the beginning of a period and a cash flow statement for that year. The question could then require the preparation of a profit and loss account and closing balance sheet from this information. Such a question would, of course, be unrealistic because anyone who had access to the cash flow statement would usually have the profit and loss account and most recent balance sheet anyway.

There is no particular secret to answering such a question. The opening balance sheet should be used as a model for the closing statement, with each figure adjusted as necessary for the transactions listed in the cash flow statement and its related notes. It should not be difficult to derive the profit and loss account from the cash flow statement although the figures will have to be adjusted to reflect the accruals as at the beginning and the end of the year.

Progress Test 3

The following pieces of information have been salvaged from the dustbin of OPQ plc by an industrial spy. OPQ is a competitor of your employer. It is unlikely to publish its latest financial statements for several weeks.

OPQ plc Draft Cash Flow Statement for the Year Ended 31 December 19X8

	£000	£000
Net cash inflow from operating activities		148
Returns on investment and servicing of finance		
Interest paid	(11)	
Dividends paid	(18)	
		(29)
Taxation		
Corporation tax paid		(66)
Investing activities		
Payments to acquire tangible fixed assets	(120)	
Payments incurred in respect of		
closure of branch	(22)	
Receipts from sale of tangible fixed assets	50	
		(92)
Net cash outflow before financing		(39)
Financing		
Issue of ordinary shares	60	
Issue of debentures	10	
		70
Increase in cash and cash equivalents		31

Notes to cash flow statement

1. Reconciliation of operating profit to net cash inflow from operations

	£000
Operating profit	131
Depreciation	40
Amortisation of goodwill	26
Gain on disposal of fixed assets	(19)
Increase in stocks	(14)
Decrease in debtors	11
Decrease in creditors	(27)
Net cash inflow from operating activities	148

2. Analysis of change in cash and cash equivalents during the year

	£000
Balance at 31 December 19X7	(20)
Net cash inflow	31
Balance at 31 December 19X8	11

3. Analysis of the balances of cash and cash equivalents as shown in the balance sheet

	19X8	19X7	Change
	£000	£000	£000
Cash at bank	11	–	11
Bank overdraft	–	(20)	20
	11	(20)	31

4. Analysis of changes in finance during the year

	Share capital £000	Share premium £000	Debenture loan £000
Balance at 31 December 19X7	200	80	120
Cash inflows from financing	50	10	10
Balance at 31 December 19X8	250	90	130

The following balance sheet was obtained from OPQ plc's previous year's annual report.

OPQ plc Balance Sheet as at 31 December 19X7

	£000	£000
Fixed Assets		
Intangible Assets		157
Tangible Assets		
Land and Buildings	210	
Plant and Machinery	180	
Fixtures and Fittings	90	
		480
		637
Current Assets		
Stocks	180	
Debtors	66	
ACT Recoverable	4	
	250	
Creditors: Amounts falling due within one year		
Bank Overdraft	(20)	
Trade Creditors	(92)	
Taxation	(64)	
Dividends	(12)	
	(188)	
Net Current Assets		62
Total Assets, Less Current Liabilities		699
Creditors: Amounts falling due after more than one year		
Debentures		(120)
		579
Capital and Reserves		
Called-up Share Capital		200
Share Premium Account		80
Revaluation Reserve		140
Profit and Loss Account		159
		579

The following information is also relevant:

1. The depreciation charge can be analysed as follows:

	£000
Land and Buildings	5
Plant and Machinery	22
Fixtures and Fittings	13
	40

2.   Plant and machinery which had a net book value of £31,000 was sold during the year and replaced with more modern equipment costing £120,000.

3.   Land and buildings were revalued by £170,000.

4.   The tax charge on ordinary activities has been estimated at £59,000.

5.   The closure costs are to be treated as an extraordinary expense. It is expected that tax relief of £8,000 will be obtained on these costs.

6   A final dividend of £18,000 was proposed at the year end.

7.   The basic rate of income tax is 25%.

From this information, you are required to prepare a balance sheet for OPQ plc as at 31 December 19X8, and a profit and loss account for the year ended 31 December 19X8, starting with profit on ordinary activities before tax.

Solution to Progress Test 3

OPQ plc Profit and Loss Account for the Year Ended 31 December 19X8

	£000	£000
Operating Profit		131
Interest Payable		(11)
Profit on Ordinary Activities		120
Tax on Profit on Ordinary Activities		(59)
Profit on Ordinary Activities after Taxation		61
Extraordinary Items		(14)
Profit for the Financial Year		47
Dividends		(24)
Profit Retained for the Year		23
Retained Profits brought forward		159
Retained Profits carried forward		182

OPQ plc Balance Sheet as at 31 December 19X8

	£000	£000
Fixed Assets		
Intangible Assets		131
Tangible Assets		
Land and Buildings	375	
Plant and Machinery	247	
Fixtures and Fittings	77	

	£000	£000
		699
		830
Current Assets		
Stocks	194	
Debtors	55	
ACT Recoverable	6	
Cash at Bank	11	
	266	
Creditors: Amounts falling due within one year		
Trade Creditors	(65)	
Taxation	(51)	
Dividends	(18)	
	(134)	
Net Current Assets		132
Total Assets less Current Liabilities		962
Creditors: Amounts falling due after more than one year		
Debentures		(130)
		832
Capital and Reserves		
Called-up Share Capital		250
Share Premium Account		90
Revaluation Reserve		310
Profit and Loss Account		182
		832

Workings

Dividends
£18,000 was paid during the year. A liability of £12,000 appeared in the balance sheet as at 31 December 19X7. It would appear that an interim dividend of £6,000 has been paid during the year.

Corporation tax
£66,000 was paid to the Inland Revenue during the year. This amount corresponds to the liability on the opening balance sheet plus the ACT on the interim dividend (i.e. £6,000 × 25/75 = £2,000).

Fixed assets
Intangible   £157,000 − 26,000 = 131,000
Land and Buildings £210,000 + 170,000 − 5,000 = 375,000

Plant and Machinery   £180,000 – 31,000 + 120,000 – 22,000 = 247,000
Fixtures and Fittings   £90,000 – 13,000 = £77,000

Tax liability

	£000	
Charge on Ordinary Activities	59	
Relief on Extraordinary Items	(8)	
ACT paid during the year:		
On 19X7 final dividend	(4)	
On 19X8 interim dividend	(2)	(see above)
MCT due within one year	45	
ACT on 19X8 final dividend	6	
	51	

Summary

The cash flow statement summarises the inflows and outflows of cash which have occurred during a period. It supplements the information given in the profit and loss account and balance sheet. The statement is not required by law. The rules governing its publication and the format which it must take are contained in FRS 1.

FRS 1 lays down a mandatory format and lists the notes which must be provided. The statement has to show cash flows under each of the following headings:

* operating activities
* returns on investment and servicing of finance
* taxation
* investing activities
* financing

Questions could be more inventive than merely requiring the preparation of the cash flow statement itself. It would, for example, be possible to set a question which started with the opening balance sheet and statement of cash flows and required the preparation of a profit and loss account and closing balance sheet from these.

Index

accounting policies, 76
Accounting Standards Board (ASB), 49, 194
Accounting Standards Committee (ASC), 49
accrued expenses, 11–12, 38
acid test ratio (*see* quick assets ratio)
acquisition method of consolidation, 115
advance corporation tax (ACT), 87–93, 97, 106, 204
assets, 1, 2, 7, 8
auditor's remuneration, 62

bad debts, 38–9
balance sheet, 21–4, 195
   statutory format, 53
balance sheet equation, 1–5,

capital, 1, 2, 7, 8, 23–4
capital reserve (on consolidation), 123, 125
cash book, 159–61
Companies Act 1985, 48, 50, 51, 60, 62, 81, 105, 116, 129, 145
Companies Act 1989, 48, 62
computerised accounting systems, 168–9
consolidated balance sheet, 117–18
consolidated profit and loss account, 145–9
corporation tax, 78–9
cost of control account, 124
cost of sales, 19–20
credit, 7, 8, 9
creditors' ledger control account (*see* purchase ledger control account)
creditors' turnover ratio, 181
current assets, 22–3
current liabilities, 23
current ratio, 177–8

debit, 7, 8, 9
debtors' control account (*see* sales ledger control account)
debtors' turnover ratio, 180, 181
deferred taxation, 89, 104–6, 204
depreciation, 28–31, 61, 70–1, 205
despatch note, 155
directors' emoluments, 61, 62–4
disposals of fixed assets, 31–3
dividends, 21, 40, 87
dual aspect concept, 5–6

efficiency ratios, 179–82
employees, 61
equity method of consolidation, 115
exceptional items, 64–5, 207
expenses, 2, 7, 8, 18
extraordinary items, 64–5, 80–1, 207

Financial Reporting Council, 49
Financial Reporting Standards (FRSs), 48, 49
financial structure, 185–7
fixed assets, 22–3, 28–33, 70–1
format 1, 51
format 2, 51, 52
formats, 50–4
franked investment income (FII), 90–1
fraud, 158
FRS 1, 194, 195, 198, 200

gearing ratio, 185–7
general ledger (*see* nominal ledger)
goods received note, 158
goodwill, 123–7, 139
gross profit, 18–19
gross profit percentage, 176

hire charges, 61
holding company, 116

income, 2, 7, 8, 18
incomplete records, 12–13

inter-company balances, 133–5
interest cover, 187
irrecoverable ACT, 97

journal entries, 9–10, 18, 38, 166

liability, 1, 2, 7, 8, 23
liquidity ratios, 177–9
long term liabilities, 23

mainstream corporation tax (MCT), 89
merger method of consolidation, 115
minority interest, 128–31

net profit, 18
net profit percentage, 176–7
nominal ledger, 10, 154, 155, 156, 160
notes, 37, 60–5

ordinary share capital, 23

pre-acquisition profits, 118–20
preference shares, 23, 40
prepaid expenses, 11–12, 38
profit and loss account, 18–21, 195
profitability ratios, 174–7
purchase day book, 158
purchase invoice, 158
purchase ledger, 158, 160
purchase ledger control account, 158

quick assets ratio, 178–9

redundancy costs, 64
Registrar of Companies, 47
research and development, 62
reserves, 24
return on capital employed, 174–5
revaluation of assets on consolidation, 139–42
revaluation reserve, 70–1

sales day book, 155, 156, 157
sales invoice, 155
sales ledger, 155, 156, 157, 160
sales ledger control account, 156, 158
segregation of duties, 159, 160
share capital, 23–4
share premium, 24
SSAP 1, 115
SSAP 2, 76
SSAP 6, 64
SSAP 8, 87, 89, 91, 97, 106
SSAP 10, 194
SSAP 13, 62
SSAP 14, 115
SSAP 15, 104, 106
SSAP 22, 123, 125, 139
SSAP 23, 115
statement of source and application of funds, 194
Statements of Standard Accounting Practice (SSAPs), 48, 49
Stock Exchange, 49
stock turnover ratio, 179–80, 181
subsidiary company, 116, 118

T accounts, 1, 6–9, 10–15, 29, 31, 32, 124, 203
tax credits, 90–1
trial balance, 10, 16–17

unrealised profits, 135–6

value added tax (VAT), 155, 158, 200

working capital cycle, 181